Woodall's

CAMPSITE
COOKBOOK

Edited by MARILYN A. BARTMESS

Cover Design: Dave Mounce, Woodall Pub. Corp

CONTENTS

Introduction • 7

1 A Word About Nutrition • 9
2 The Camp Kitchen • 12
3 Pots, Pans and the Pantry • 16
4 Fire Building • 21
5 Aluminum Foil Cooking • 27
6 Reflector Oven Cooking • 51
7 Dutch Oven Cooking • 68
8 Breads and Breakfast • 93
9 Soups and Sauces • 105
10 Salads, Dressings and Relishes • 116
11 Vegetable Dishes • 136
12 Cooking Inside Your Rig ... Casseroles and
   Skillet Meals • 148
13 Grilling and Barbecuing • 170
14 Campsite Desserts • 194
15 Campfire Snacks • 216
16 Beverages • 231
17 Camp Cooking Hints • 246
   Index • 253

Introduction

CAMPSITE COOKING *doesn't have to be limited to half-burnt hot dogs with a side of pork 'n' beans. Great campsite cooking can be achieved with little more than an adventurous attitude and a few of the recipes found in this classic cookbook. From traditional Dutch Irish Stew (page 72) to easy Peanut Butter Fudge (page 227), the recipes in this cookbook are timeless. I guarantee that every member of your family will find a new favorite!*

So what will you find in this classic set of recipes? Special instructions on everything from nutrition to stocking the camp kitchen; from using your Dutch Oven to successfully cooking over open coals. In chapter 5, for example, the easy and efficient method of aluminum foil cooking is explored and dozens of recipes are recommended. Cooking food in a tightly sealed foil package is like cooking in a miniature pressure cooker. The food cooks rapidly over a coal grill or an open fire, basted with steam from its own juices. The steaming action even retains essential vitamins and minerals and increases the digestibility of some foods. Or, if you are cooking in your RV, take this method inside to the oven and enjoy an easy cleanup without messy pans to wash.

Where else can you find recipes like Spaghetti and Bones (page 80), The Fastest Sauce in the West (page 113), and my personal favorite, Roadside Spuds (page 145)? And for dessert, how about giving your kids Hairy Squares (page 226) or Butterscotch Munchers (page 218)?

No matter which recipe ends up being your favorite to prepare and enjoy, I guarantee that food around the campsite will be more fun and tastier than ever. Thank you for taking Woodall's Campsite Cookbook along with you as you take to the open road.

Sincerely,

Ann Emerson

Ann Emerson,
Associate Publisher

1
A Word About Nutrition

WHEN YOU'RE PLANNING a campsite menu, you'll want to please your family by serving them the kind of meals they enjoy. At the same time, you must be sure your family is receiving the proper nourishment for an active outdoor life.

If your camping family isn't eating a well-balanced diet, the strenuous activity of outdoor living may cause them to tire easily, be irritable or to lack stamina.

When the camp chef plans menus that contain the right amounts of the right foods, efforts will be bountifully rewarded since good nutrition enables you to be filled with energy, vitality and a sense of well-being. And, most important, it can also add healthier, happier years to your life.

A well-balanced camping diet should include foods that contain a minimum daily amount of six nutrients: proteins, carbohydrates, fats, vitamins, minerals and water.

PROTEINS: The body needs a constant supply of proteins since they are the nutrients which handle the job of building and repairing body cells. Complete protein foods include milk, eggs, cheese, meat, poultry or fish.

CARBOHYDRATES: Carbohydrates are foods which contain large amounts of sugar and starch and supply the body with quick energy. Breads, cereals, vegetables, fruits and concentrated sweets form the major source of carbohydrates in a camper's daily diet.

FATS: Fats are foods which supply a concentrated source of energy which is stored in the body. It isn't hard to guess which foods contain fats, although few foods are composed only of fats. Animal fats are found in meat, fish, poultry, milk and egg yolk; vegetable fats are contained in oils, margarine and such fruits as avocados and olives.

VITAMINS: Vitamins are important nutrients because they help regulate body processes and also help the body utilize other nutrients like proteins, fats and carbohydrates. Vitamin A promotes a clear, smooth skin; Vitamin D develops good bones and teeth; and the three Vitamins in the B complex promote good digestion, good appetite and good vision. If a camper's daily diet is balanced with essential food, however, all the vitamins will be present and vitamin supplements will not be needed.

MINERALS: Minerals are essential nutrients that we obtain through eating plants that contain them or by eating meat from animals that have previously eaten those plants. Calcium is essential for good growth of bones and teeth; phosphorus is necessary to convert protein, fat and carbohydrates into energy; iron forms hemoglobin, the red part of the blood which carries oxygen to body tissues. Foods such as milk, broccoli, salmon, oranges, baked beans and potatoes are rich in calcium; liver, egg yolk, apricots, prunes and meat are good sources of iron.

WATER: Water is the sixth nutrient, second in importance only to oxygen. It is possible to live without food for a few weeks or more, but one can live without water for only a few days.

When you consider your family's nutritional needs, remember that no single food contains all the vital nutrients and that foods vary in the amounts of nutrients they do contain. A person can be undernourished if his diet consists of too many foods that are low in nutritional value.

For example, it's all too easy for a camping diet to be high in carbohydrates, especially sweets, yet low in proteins or vitamins. Every meal need not be balanced, but a conscientious effort should be made to balance the day's total intake of food.

Recent innovations in the field of nutrition have simplified the grouping of food into four categories. Knowing these categories and the amounts of food in each group that should be eaten daily is the best key to good campsite nutrition.

A camper's daily guide to good eating should include the following:

MINIMUM DAILY REQUIREMENTS

Group 1 DAIRY FOODS	Children and teenagers: 3 or 4 glasses of milk daily; adults 2 or more glasses. Dairy products such as cheese and ice cream can supply part of the milk total.
Group 2 MEAT	2 or more servings daily: meat, fish, poultry, eggs or cheese; dried beans and peas or nuts can serve as substitutes.
Group 3 FRUITS AND VEGETABLES	4 or more servings daily: include a citrus fruit or vegetable known for Vitamin C content; a dark-green or deep-yellow vegetable for Vitamin A should be eaten at least every other day; include other fruits and vegetables, including potatoes.
Group 4 BREADS AND CEREALS	4 or more servings daily; enriched bread contains added vitamins and minerals; whole-grain bread provides added nutritional values.

2
The Camp Kitchen

In CAMP, a kitchen can be as elaborate or as simple as you wish—and it can be indoors in your camping rig or outdoors under the nearest tree.

A camp kitchen, however, should contain three basic centers of activity: a cooking center, a refrigeration center, and a cleanup center. How you organize and arrange these centers is a matter of personal taste and depends on the kind of camping equipment you use.

An Indoor Camp Kitchen

If you camp with a travel trailer, tent trailer, pickup coach, step-van or motor home, chances are your camp kitchen has been planned and organized for you.

The cooking center in a modern recreational vehicle usually consists of a built-in tabletop range and a built-in oven, both designed for a close fit with surrounding wall and floor cabinets. The range and oven are fueled by liquid petroleum gas and operate as easily as any conventional gas range. Many rigs also feature a hooded vent fan over the range which clears a camping rig of cooking odors, smoke and heat moisture.

The refrigeration center in today's camping rig has come a long way from the little icebox found in early camping trailers. Today's recreational vehicle comes with a convenient built-in refrigerator that operates on either liquid petroleum gas or electric current, and some even have a separate freezer compartment large enough to hold several days' supply of frozen food. Most models also come with hinges on both sides of the door so the camp chef can arrange her refrigerator door to open in the most convenient direction.

The cleanup center in a modern camping rig consists of a single- or a double-drain sink constructed of stainless steel or porcelain enamel. If the camping rig is equipped with an LP gas-fueled hot water heater, the sink will be equipped with either a conventional separate hot and cold water faucet or a single-handle faucet that controls both hot and cold water mixing and water volume. Many rigs also offer a retractable hand-held spray hose as an optional sink accessory.

Other kitchen features found in most modern recreational vehicles include sturdy wall and floor cabinets, durable Formica-type counters and backsplashes, efficient light fixtures and conveniently placed electric outlets. Floors are of vinyl linoleum or carpeting, walls and ceiling of prefinished vinyl-faced wood paneling or prefinished vinyl.

Like other campers who own modern camping rigs, we enjoy the luxury features of our indoor camp kitchen. However, we've discovered that if we rely on it exclusively for cooking we unwittingly fall into the trap of serving campsite meals exactly like meals served at home. To add variety to our camping menu we carry outdoor cooking gear and find that meal preparation is more fun when we use our Dutch oven, reflector oven, charcoal grill or portable camp stove.

In addition, we enjoy tinkering with the challenging art of campfire cooking and tend to agree with old-timers who claim that good outdoor cooking can only be done on a wood fire.

So—no matter how efficient your indoor camp kitchen may be—to add a new dimension to camp cooking we suggest preparing at least one meal a day using outdoor cooking gear.

An Outdoor Camp Kitchen

If you travel light, and if your home in the great outdoors is a tent or a sleeping bag, in order to prepare nutritious campsite meals you'll need to set up an outdoor camp kitchen. You can organize your three basic kitchen centers by selecting gear from the wide variety of equipment available at all camping supply centers.

The cooking center. Although backpackers and woodsmen may cook three meals a day over a campfire, for a quick, instant cooking flame a useful piece of equipment is a two- or a three-burner camp stove, fueled either by LP gas or white gasoline. Such stoves may be obtained with a folding stand to bring them to convenient kitchen range height.

Another item that's useful to the outdoor chef is a portable oven designed to be used with a camp stove that burns white gasoline or a special fuel canned under the manufacturer's label. Our family has owned a portable oven for years and finds it especially handy for baking casserole dishes or heating bakery goods.

The refrigeration center. To keep food at its nutritious best, store perishables in an insulated cooler chest. The most popular chests are constructed of metal or Styrofoam and they come in a wide assortment of shapes and sizes. One of the largest chests on the market has a 68-quart capacity and holds a 25-pound cake of ice—enough to keep food fresh for several days. However, if you plan to buy a large cooler look for one with a drain spout for the melted ice runoff. Then, to conserve space in your chest, store drinking water or other beverages in an insulated picnic jug.

For the ultimate in outdoor refrigeration, and if money is no object, you can outfit your camp kitchen with a portable 12/110-volt refrigerator with an adapter that plugs into an automobile cigarette lighter. Portable refrigerators range in size from one to four cubic feet and cost anywhere from $50 to $150.

The clean-up center. Although rugged types prefer to wash and rinse utensils using two pails of water heated over a camp-fire, we clean up with a divided plastic mop bucket that holds both the sudsy and the rinse water, and we heat the water on our stove. For more luxurious pot washing, you can buy a portable plastic sink that comes with a hand pump, a water tap and a hose that attaches to a water jug. We've never used a portable sink but it looks like a handy addition to any outdoor kitchen.

Once you've assembled all the gear for the three basic centers of an outdoor kitchen you'll need a cupboard or a "chuck box" to stow it in. You can improvise a chuck box from a large cardboard container, you can build one from plywood, or you can buy one ready-made. There are several commercial cupboards available and some may be purchased in kit form. Most come with a counter door, a gadget drawer and three or four storage compartments. At camp they can be placed at one end of a picnic table or set up on a folding stand.

Cooking in an outdoor kitchen is fun—if you've got the right equipment. Select your gear carefully and buy quality items from manufacturers with a reputation for reliability. And remember—you're investing in gear that will make your family's camping holidays more comfortable and more convenient for many years to come.

3
Pots, Pans
and
the Pantry

The kind of pots and pans, paring knives or mixing bowls found in a camp kitchen are not directly related to the nutritional state of a family, but they do exert an indirect influence.

If large enough pots aren't available, if pot lids don't fit, if pans scorch foods too easily or are difficult to clean, the camp chef can become discouraged and spend her time figuring ways to get the job over and done with.

Since mealtime in camp should be a happy occasion for everyone, including the chef, lighten camp-cooking chores by carrying utensils and equipment that are equal to, if not better than, the ones used in your kitchen at home.

If your camping rig has plenty of storage room, it's a good idea to purchase utensils and table service, label them "camping," and store them permanently in your unit.

Campers who depend on a chuck box to keep their utensils together will find a set of nested cooking pots a practical investment. The pots found in these kits usually have lids with detachable handles that double as frying pans, and all fit into one large kettle for compact storage.

There are countless additional items available to make camp cooking easier and more convenient. In fact, there is so much equipment to choose from, a camper can become bewildered as to the best choices.

To help the camp chef select the equipment needed for efficient preparation of campsite meals, we offer a check list of items which we consider basic to any camp kitchen.

Basic Equipment

Table Service and Storage

Plastic tablecloth
Plates, cups, glasses
Cereal and dessert bowls
Meat platter and serving dish

Knives, forks, spoons
Tablespoons
Plastic food containers
Plastic juice containers

Disposables

Paper towels
Paper napkins
Garbage bags
Aluminum foil

Waxed paper
Disposable plates, glasses, cups, table service (optional), foil pans (optional)

For Cooking

Coffeepot
Fry pans
Saucepans
Griddle
Pancake turner
Egg beater
Potato masher
Soup pot
Soup ladle
Long-handled spoons and forks
Ice pick

Mixing bowls
Measuring cups and spoons
Hot pads
Large strainer
Tongs
Can and bottle openers
Paring knife
Carving knives
Potato peeler
Matches
Cookbook

If your camping rig has an oven, or if you pack a portable camp oven, you'll need to carry:

Roasting pan (small)
Cookie sheet
Pie pan

Baking pan (small)
Muffin tins
Casserole dish

For outdoor cooking, pack:

Portable camp stove with fuel
    supply and small funnel
Dutch oven
Reflector oven

Barbecue grill and charcoal
Vacuum bottle
Water jug
Ice chest

Clean-up Equipment

Detergent
Scouring pads
Cleanser

Dishcloth and towels
Plastic dishpan or sink
Plastic dish drainer

After preparing more than a thousand compsite meals, our family has finally compiled a check list of basic, nonperishable food items that we consider essential to planning nutritious campsite meals. Included in our list are sauces and seasonings that make foods more interesting and appealing.

Of course, we don't rely on our basic food supply for three meals a day. We find that camping gives us a perfect opportunity to learn about different types of food grown in each section of our country. Thus, to augment our food supply when we're camping, we shop for fresh and regional foods along the way.

We offer our list as a guide and hope it will be helpful when you stock your camp pantry.

THE PANTRY

Prepared mixes:

Biscuit
Pancake
Cake and frosting
Pie crust

Dried soup
Instant mashed potatoes
Muffin
Packaged dinners

Powdered foods:

Milk
Hot chocolate
Cocoa
Instant coffee
Instant tea

Fruit juice
Gelatin
Pudding
Pie filling

Staples:

Baking powder
Baking soda
Cereal
Coffee
Dried fruits (apricots, dates,
   prunes, raisins)
Flour (all-purpose)
Marshmallows

Noodles (spaghetti, macaroni)
Onions
Popping corn
Potatoes
Rice
Shortening
Sugar (granulated, brown)

In jars or cans:

Beef stew
Chicken
Chili con carne
Chinese noodles
Chipped beef
Chow mein
Cooking oil

Corned beef
Evaporated milk
Fruit
Gravy
Ham
Jam and jelly
Juice (vegetable, fruit)

Mayonnaise
Molasses
Peanut butter
Soup
Spaghetti sauce
Syrup (maple, chocolate)

Tomato paste
Tomato sauce
Tuna
Vegetables
Vienna sausage

Food adjuncts:

Catsup
Cream of tartar
Extracts (vanilla, lemon)
Flakes (celery, onion)
Garlic
Herbs (bay leaf, parsley)
Lemon juice
Mustard
Pickles
Meat tenderizer
Powders (garlic, onion, curry)

Salt
Seasoned salts (onion, garlic, celery)
Sauces (chili, Worcestershire Tabasco)
Spices (cinnamon, ginger, nutmeg, paprika, pepper oregano)
Vinegar
Monosodium glutamate

4
Fire
Building

To BUILD A FIRE, to strike a match and to watch the flames leap up and lick the wood are all part of the thrill of camping. Yet there's a lot more to successfully starting a "one matcher" than just tossing a lighted match at a pile of dry twigs. To help you get your fire started here are a few suggestions.

If your campsite doesn't have an established fireplace, and if you have permission to build a campfire, select a spot that is in an open area away from trees or low-hanging branches.

Clear a circle of all leaves, twigs or other combustible materials and build a fireplace on the ground by placing rocks around the rim of your circle. If you're building a cooking fire, confine the circle to the size of your grill. Don't use shale, slate or schist for your fireplace rim since these rocks are formed in layers, and when heated the moisture within them produces steam which can cause them to explode.

Lay a pile of tinder on the ground in the center of your fireplace, and over it place a generous amount of kindling. Light the tinder and after the fire is burning, add fuel.

The kind of tinder, kindling and fuel that's available for your campfire depends on where you are camping. Generally, most campground owners provide bundled firewood for a nominal sum, but if you're looking for these materials yourself you should know what to look for.

Tinder may be dead twigs from standing trees, bark from dead trees, finely split piñon pine or pine needles. Our favorite tinder happens to be a crumpled-up newspaper.

Kindling is made by chopping firewood into small pieces or by using small branches from dead trees.

Fuel is simply firewood—and the kind of fuel you burn determines how hot or how long lasting your campfire will be.

Arranging your tinder, kindling and fuel so that the fire burns properly is an easy matter. Our favorite fire is called the teepee, and we make it by placing kindling around tinder in a conical shape resembling an Indian tipi, or tepee. If we plan to cook with a fire, we support our grate by building a teepee fire between two logs about three feet long.

Teepee fires built with softwoods are good for reflector oven cooking, which depends on a high, steady flame. A teepee fire built with hardwood, gives coals that are good for Dutch oven cooking.

Our Scouting daughters enjoy constructing a more elaborate campfire called a Log Cabin, and they build it by crisscrossing logs over a bed of tinder and kindling.

Trench fires are also used for cooking and they're easy to build. Dig a trench about one foot deep by about three feet long. Lay a good bed of tinder and kindling in the bottom of the trench and add fuel after the kindling is burning. Trench fires are useful for cooking on a windy day, but don't fill the trench opening with too many pots or pans or you won't have enough draft to keep the fire going.

Since most campers cover a lot of territory during their camping trips, it might be a good idea to learn which firewoods are available in the different sections of our country.

There are six major forest areas in the United States and they contain 1,182 species of trees, which fall into two basic categories—deciduous and conifers.

Most deciduous trees are hardwoods with broad leaves which are shed in the fall. These trees remain dormant during the winter and they provide the best woods for a cooking fire. Hardwoods burn clean and slowly and leave lots of good hot cooking coals. Use them when you're cooking with a Dutch oven or roasting food in aluminum foil.

Most conifers are evergreens, or softwoods, and they produce seeds within cones. Conifers usually have needles which they shed, but not all at once, and they remain green throughout the year. Softwoods light easily and make a good campfire, but they burn fast and leave few coals. Use softwoods for reflector oven cooking.

If you live on the Pacific coast, anywhere from Alaska to California, it will be difficult to find hardwood for your campfire since one of the largest coniferous forests in the world runs through this area and it includes the largest trees in the world— the redwoods.

East of this forest lies another forest of mainly coniferous trees that covers the Rocky Mountains from Canada to Mexico. The western forest consists of ponderosa pine, Douglas fir, Englemann spruce and other conifers, and among the few deciduous trees found in the area are aspen and cottonwood.

A mixed forest containing both hardwood and softwood trees is found along the northern edge of our country from New England through Minnesota, dipping down into West Virginia, Kentucky, Tennessee and North Carolina. Coniferous trees in this forest are the red or Norway pine, the jack pine, white pine, spruce and fir. Hardwood trees include the maple, birch, and beech.

The largest forest of all ranges from the Atlantic coast to beyond the Mississippi River and it's mainly a deciduous forest with many hardwood trees, including beech, oak, hickory, elm, ash and walnut.

The beautiful southern forest covers a large area extending from the Atlantic coast through Louisiana, and it's composed mainly of conifers, although such hardwoods as oak, willow, cottonwood, ash, pecan and poplar may also be found.

The sixth major forest is a tropical one and lies chiefly at the southern tip of Florida and along the southern Gulf coast of

Texas. Hardwood trees in this forest are mahogany, mangrove, and bay.

For a handy reference to the best-known hardwood and softwood trees, we've compiled a list showing the general areas of our country where they may be found.

DECIDUOUS TREES

Alder, red—*Pacific coast*
Apple—*east; central; northern; southern*
Ash—*east; central; southern*
Aspen—*Rocky Mountain; northern*
Bay—*tropical*
Beech—*east; central; northern*
Birch—*northern*
Chestnut—*east; central*
Cottonwood—*Pacific coast; Rocky Mountain; east, central, southern*
Dogwood—*east; central*
Elm—*east; central*
Gum, black—*east; central; southern*
Gum, red—*east; central; southern*
Hickory—*east; central*
Locust—*east; central*
Mahogany—*tropical*
Mahogany, mountain—*Rocky Mountain*
Mangrove—*tropical*
Maple, bigleaf—*Pacific coast*
Maple, red—*east; central; northern*
Maple, sugar—*northern*
Oak—*east; central; northern; southern*
Pecan—*southern*
Poplar—*east; central; southern*
Sycamore—*east; central*
Tulip—*east; central*

Walnut—*east; central*
Willow—*southern*

Coniferous Trees

Cedar, incense—*Pacific coast; Rocky Mountain*
Cedar, red—*Pacific coast; Rocky Mountain; east; central*
Cedar, white—*northern*
Cyprus—*southern*
Fir, balsam—*Pacific coast; northern*
Fir, Douglas—*Pacific coast; Rocky Mountain*
Fir, white—*Rocky Mountain; northern*
Hemlock,—*northern*
Hemlock, western—*Pacific coast*
Larch, western—*Rocky Mountain*
Loblolly—*southern*
Pine, jack—*northern*
Pine, longleaf—*southern*
Pine, lodgepole—*Rocky Mountain*
Pine, ponderosa—*Rocky Mountain*
Pine, red—*northern*
Pine, shortleaf—*east; central; southern*
Pine, slash—*southern*
Pine, sugar—*Pacific coast; Rock Mountain*
Pine, Virginia—*east; central*
Pine, white—*Rocky Mountain; east; central; northern*
Redwood—*Pacific coast*
Spruce, Englemann—*Rocky Mountain*
Spruce, northern—*northern*
Spruce, Sitka—*Pacific coast*
Tamarack—*northern*

REMEMBER: Nine out of ten forest fires are caused by human carelessness. After you've built your fire and enjoyed its cheery warmth, be sure it's completely out before you leave the campsite. Pour water on it, stir it up and then pour more water on to be sure it's dead. If your fire isn't in an established fireplace, bury the dead coals or cover them with sand.

5
Aluminum Foil
Cooking

WHEN WE'RE CAMPED in the shadow of a jagged snow-covered mountain peak, or on a site overlooking a crystal-clear fishing lake, we move our kitchen outdoors so we can enjoy the dramatic scenery to the fullest, even as we prepare meals.

And to satisfy hearty outdoor appetites we prepare many fast and filling meals using aluminum foil and coals from our charcoal grill or our campfire.

We've learned there's a whole new world of delectable and flavorful eating wrapped in shiny aluminum foil, and surprisingly, we've also discovered that foil-cooked foods are often easier to digest and more nutritious than foods prepared in a conventional way.

Aluminum foil comes in two weights: all-purpose and heavy duty, which is marketed as "broiling, cooking and freezing foil." Both types of foil are easily obtained in most supermarkets.

When cooking on coals with all-purpose foil, use a double thickness. When cooking with heavy-duty foil, a single thickness is usually sufficient.

Cooking food in a tightly sealed foil package is somewhat like cooking in a miniature pressure cooker. The food cooks rapidly by itself, basted with steam from its own juices, or a marinade, and very little moisture escapes. This "steaming" action retains essential vitamins and minerals and increases the digestibility of some foods.

The secret to successful foil cooking is a well-sealed package and, unless you're cooking a large roast, wrapping each serving individually. When using all-purpose foil, cut two squares and use a double thickness for each package. When using heavy-duty foil, a single thickness is sufficient.

When we prepare a campsite meal with foil, we lightly grease the surface of a large square of heavy-duty foil with cooking oil to keep the food from sticking after cooking. We place the food in the center, then add seasoning and, if the recipe calls for it, a liquid, sauce or a marinade.

For a tightly sealed package we recommend using a drugstore wrap. Bring the two opposite sides of the foil up and around the food, pinch the edges together and fold the double seam down two or three times until it rests snugly on the package. Seal the ends in the same fashion and place the package on medium-hot coals that have been tempered with ashes.

Because I am a somewhat absentminded cook who tends to wander off from the campfire, I have burned more than my share of foil-cooked dinners. To gain a few extra minutes cooking time in case I decide to take an unscheduled hike, I often wrap larger cuts of meat or poultry in a double thickness of heavy-duty foil. The extra layer of heavy-duty foil isn't necessary, however, and only serves to slow down cooking time a bit.

I can also slow down cooking time a few more minutes by placing foil packages on a grill three or four inches above the hot coals. However, food wrapped in heavy-duty foil, or in two thicknesses of all-purpose foil, can be buried in the coals, placed beside the coals or on the coals as well as on a grill—it all depends on your own personal judgment.

To determine if the coals are hot enough for cooking, hold your hand over them at cooking height. The number of seconds you can keep your hand over the coals will tell you how hot they are. Two to three seconds—hot; four to five seconds—medium hot. Recipes in this chapter are timed approximately for medium hot coals.

Estimating exact cooking times for foil-cooked foods is a skill that has to be learned with practice. Pinching or probing the packages with a fork to see if the food is ready for the table could lead to a loss of cooking liquid. If you've wrapped the food using a drugstore fold, it's just as easy to open the package and see for yourself.

Practically anything becomes outdoor fare when it's cooked in aluminum foil, and it's an ideal way to prepare the less tender cuts of meat that require long cooking time with moist heat.

If you're tired of grilling franks or "burgers," and if your budget rejects steak every night, cook outdoors with aluminum foil and serve your family flavorful dishes that are easy to cook, easy to clean up and easy on the budget.

FOIL-COOKED VEGETABLES

To keep your family physically healthy and mentally alert, balance their diet with daily servings of fresh vegetables. Once they've tasted fresh vegetables cooked in aluminum foil, no enticement will be needed to get them to eat foods that are really good for them!

For individual servings of . . .

CARROTS

Pare and slice 3 carrots and place slices on lightly oiled square of heavy-duty foil. Add butter and seasoning. Seal package and place on medium-hot coals for about 15 minutes, or until tender.

CORN I

Remove husk and silk from corn. Brush ears with melted butter or margarine, season with salt and pepper. Wrap each ear separately in lightly greased heavy-duty foil, seal packages and place on medium-hot coals for about 30 minutes, turning occasionally.

CORN II

Blend 1 envelope dried onion soup mix with ½ pound soft margarine. Brush prepared ears of corn with mixture. Wrap and cook as above.

INDIAN CORN

Pull back husks, remove silk and place corn in pan of cold water for about 30 minutes. Remove, drain and brush ears with melted butter or margarine. Replace husk and wrap each ear in lightly oiled square of heavy-duty foil. Seal package and place on medium-hot coals for about 30 minutes, turning occasionally.

GREEN BEANS

Clean beans and place 8 whole beans on a lightly oiled square of heavy-duty foil, add butter and season with salt and pepper. Seal package and place on medium-hot coals for about 15 minutes, or until tender.

MUSHROOMS

Dip 12 large mushrooms in salad oil. Place on large lightly oiled square of heavy-duty foil and season with salt and pepper. Seal package and place on medium-hot coals for 15 minutes. (Makes 4 servings)

ONIONS

Peel onions, slice and place slices on lightly oiled heavy-duty foil square. Add butter and seasoning. Seal package and place over coals for about 20 minutes.

PEAS

Place ½ cup shelled peas on lightly oiled heavy-duty foil square. Add butter and seasoning. Seal package and place on medium-hot coals for about 15 minutes.

BAKED POTATOES I

Scrub large baking potato; pierce with fork. Wrap in lightly oiled heavy-duty foil square and place sealed package on medium-hot coals for about 45 minutes, or until soft.

BAKED POTATOES II

After scrubbing baking potato, slice in half and season with salt and pepper. Place a pat of butter on top of each half, wrap in lightly oiled heavy-duty foil and place sealed package on medium-hot coals for about 45 minutes.

SLICED POTATOES I

Pare one large baking potato and slice into ⅛-inch-thick slices. Place slices on lightly oiled square of heavy-duty foil, add butter and seasoning. Seal package and place on medium-hot coals for about 30 minutes.

SLICED POTATOES II

Peel and slice one onion and add to potato slices. Add butter and seasoning. Wrap in greased heavy-duty foil, seal and place on medium-hot coals for about 30 minutes.

SLICED POTATOES III

After scrubbing, paring and slicing potatoes, place slices on large lightly oiled squares of heavy-duty foil. Cover with a mixture of ½ cup soft butter blended with 1 envelope of dried onion soup mix. Seal packages and place on medium-hot coals for about 1 hour.

SWEET POTATOES

Scrub sweet potatoes and pierce with fork. Wrap in lightly oiled squares of heavy-duty foil, seal package and place on medium-hot coals for about 45 minutes, or until soft.

SQUASH

Cut squash in half. Clean and score inside with knife. Rub in butter and sprinkle with salt and pepper. Wrap each half in lightly oiled square of heavy-duty foil and place sealed packages on medium-hot coals for about 30 minutes, or until soft.

STUFFED SQUASH

After halving and scoring squash, fill with 1 can corned beef hash. Dot with butter and season. Wrap in greased heavy-duty foil, seal package and place on medium-hot coals about 30 minutes.

TOMATOES

Wash tomatoes and halve. Dot each half with butter or margarine, season with salt and pepper. Wrap two halves in lightly oiled squares of heavy-duty foil, seal and place package on medium-hot coals for about 20 minutes. If desired, sprinkle each tomato half with grated Romano cheese before cooking.

Serve potatoes "family style" and eliminate pot washing by cooking them in a disposable foil pan. The following recipe is a flavorful variation of an old campers' standby—scalloped potatoes—and it comes to us from Master Campfire Chef Mrs. R. Dean Johnson of Ashland, Wisconsin. Mrs. Johnson won first prize with her recipe in the vegetable catergory of our recent Open Fire Camp Cooking contest.

CHEESIE POTATOES

6 baking potatoes
½ pound American cheese, cubed
½ small onion, minced
1 teaspoon salt
dash pepper
3 tablespoons margarine or butter
½ cup light cream
¼ cup milk

Grease disposable 10-inch-square foil pan. Place layers of potatoes, cheese and onion in pan. Season with salt and pepper, dot with margarine or butter. Pour cream and milk over all. Seal pan with square of heavy-duty aluminum foil and place on medium-hot coals for about 1 hour, or until tender. Serves 4 to 6.

You can cook up a delicious vegetable course even at the most remote campsite if you pack instant mashed potatoes. For extra flavor, season them with onion flakes. For a gourmet touch, prepare them this way.

DEVILED POTATOES

package of instant mashed potatoes	½ teaspoon salt
½ cup of sour cream	½ teaspoon sugar
2 teaspoons prepared mustard	2 tablespoons chopped onion, or onion flakes

Prepare 4 servings of instant mashed potatoes according to directions on the package. Heat sour cream, add mustard, salt and sugar and stir mixture into hot potatoes. Add onion or onion flakes. Place individual portions on lightly oiled squares of heavy-duty aluminum foil, sprinkle with paprika if desired. Seal package and place on medium-hot coals for about 25 minutes. (If using onion flakes, shorten cooking time.)

Second prize in the vegetable category of our 1969 Open Fire Camp Cooking contest was awarded to Master Campfire Chef Mrs. John Burnham, who submitted the following recipe for Pizza Tomatoes.

PIZZA TOMATOES

4 or 5 ripe tomatoes	10 brown-and-serve sausages
oregano	Mozzarella cheese, sliced

Split tomatoes into thirds and arrange cut-side up on large lightly oiled squares of heavy-duty aluminum foil. Sprinkle with oregano and top with sliced brown-and-serve sausages. Add cheese slices and additional oregano if desired. Seal package and place on medium-hot coals for about 15 or 20 minutes. Serves 4.

Whether they're eaten raw or cooked, tomatoes are packed with essential vitamins necessary for a well-balanced diet. Serve them often and in a variety of ways.

CHEESIE TOMATOES

5 ripe tomatoes
salt and pepper
¼ cup soft bread crumbs
¼ cup American cheese, shredded

1 tablespoon butter or margarine, melted
snipped parsley or chives, optional

Slice tops off tomatoes and cut zigzag edges. Season with salt and pepper. Blend bread crumbs with cheese and melted butter or margarine, sprinkle mixture over tomatoes. Garnish with parsley or chives if desired. Wrap in lightly oiled squares of heavy-duty foil. Seal package and place on medium-hot coals for about 15 minutes. Serves 4.

CAMPER'S CASSEROLE ITALIANO

For individual servings:

1 tomato, cubed
1 potato, sliced
1 zucchini, cubed
2 teaspoons dry onion soup mix

oregano
1 tablespoon butter or margarine

Arrange cubed tomato and potato slices with zucchini on large lightly oiled square of heavy-duty foil. Cover with remaining ingredients. Seal package and place on medium-hot coals for about 45 minutes, turning occasionally.

Zucchini Creole is a delicous dish that won third prize in our Open Fire Camp Cooking contest. The recipe was submitted by Master Campfire Chef Mrs. Art J. Hansen of Cheteck, Wisconsin.

ZUCCHINI CREOLE

zucchini squash	salt and pepper
tomatoes, cubed	sugar
celery, sliced	butter or margarine

Slice zucchini crosswise into ¼-inch-thick slices. Place individual portions on lightly oiled squares of heavy-duty foil. Add cubed tomatoes, sliced celery, salt and pepper. Sprinkle with sugar and add a pat of butter or margarine on each portion. Seal and place package on medium-hot coals for 15 to 25 minutes.

Canned vegetables are easily transported to camp—and make a tasty dish when heated over hot cooking coals.

CAMPFIRE BEANS

1 1-pound can cut green beans, drained	2 tablespoons butter or margarine
1 1-pound can cut wax beans, drained	½ teaspoon salt
	dash pepper

Mix all ingredients together and mound an individual serving in center of each large lightly oiled heavy-duty foil square. Seal packages and place on medium-hot coals for about 15 minutes.

JOHNNY APPLESEED'S BEANS

6 large apples
1 14-ounce can oven-baked
  beans

1 tablespoon orange
  marmalade

Core the center from each apple and scoop out a generous amout of pulp, leaving a firm shell. Combine beans with marmalade and fill the apples with the mixture. Place on lightly oiled squares of heavy-duty foil, wrap and seal. Place package on medium-hot coals for about 30 minutes, or until apples feel tender. Serves 6.

FOIL-COOKED RICE

Precooked rice, enriched with added vitamins, is a popular ingredient of many delicious and nutritious campsite casserole dishes. Here are three that can be prepared in aluminum foil.

BARBECUE RICE

2¼ cups precooked rice
2¼ cups water

1 tablespoon butter
¾ teaspoon salt

Measure two 18-inch-square sheets of heavy-duty foil. Place on top of one another in medium-size bowl; press down to form a pouch. Combine rice, water, butter and salt and place in foil pouch. Fold foil to seal tightly and remove pouch from bowl. Place foil pouch on medium-hot coals and cook about 7 minutes, turning occasionally. Open foil and fluff rice. Makes 4 to 6 servings.

PICNIC RICE

1⅓ cups precooked rice	2 tablespoons minced onion
1⅓ cups water	1 teaspoon prepared mustard
½ cup Cheddar cheese, grated	½ teaspoon salt
¼ cup catsup	dash pepper

Fold 32-inch-length heavy-duty aluminum foil in half; press into large bowl to form pouch. Add water, cheese, catsup, onion, mustard, salt and pepper. Blend well. Stir in rice and mix just to moisten all right. Seal pouch tightly and remove from bowl. Place foil pouch on medium-hot coals and cook for about 10 minutes. Rotate pouch and continue cooking about 10 minutes longer. Open package and fluff rice. Makes 3 to 4 servings.

ITALIAN RICE LOAF

1⅓ cups precooked rice	1 envelope garlic salad dressing mix
¼ cup finely chopped onion	1 chicken bouillon cube
2 tablespoons butter or margarine	1½ cups hot water
2 tomatoes, cut in wedges	2 tablespoons grated Parmesan cheese

Shape a 15-inch sheet of 12-inch wide heavy-duty aluminum foil to resemble a loaf of Italian bread. Leave long edges open across top and close short ends by twisting. Place onion and butter in foil loaf. Add tomatoes and sprinkle with 1½ teaspoons salad dressing mix. Add rice. Dissolve chicken bouillon cube in hot water, add to rice. Seal top edges of foil by folding together. Place package on medium-hot coals for about 10 minutes. Remove package, open and fluff rice. Close package and place back on coals and continue cooking 5 minutes longer. Stir in cheese before serving. Makes 4 servings.

FOIL-COOKED MEAT

Everyone needs at least two daily servings of meat, or the nutritional equivalent, in order to maintain a diet that is high in protein content. Less expensive cuts of meat can be cooked to a tender goodness in aluminum foil over hot cooking coals.

FOIL POT ROAST

3 to 4 pounds beef pot roast
salt and pepper

1 can condensed mushroom
  soup

Place roast on large square of double-thick heavy-duty foil. Lightly oil inner cooking square. Season with salt and pepper and cover with soup. Seal package and place on medium-hot coals for about 3 hours. Turn meat every 30 minutes. After 2 hours of cooking, open package and check for doneness. Rewrap and continue cooking until meat is tender. Serves 6 to 8.

ONION ROAST

3 to 4 pounds chuck roast
salt and pepper
1 envelope onion soup mix

1 4-ounce can sliced
   mushrooms, drained

Place meat in center of a large lightly oiled square of double-thick heavy-duty foil. Season with salt and pepper. Sprinkle soup mix over meat and cover with drained mushrooms. Seal package and place on medium-hot coals for about 2 hours, or until tender. Serves 6 to 8.

CHUCK WAGON STEAK

1 3 to 4 pound chuck steak
¼ cup water
1½ tablespoons meat
   tenderizer

MARINADE
⅓ cup honey
⅓ cup lemon juice
¼ cup soy sauce
2 cloves garlic, crushed
½ teaspoon hot pepper sauce

Combine marinade ingredients, blending well. Moisten both sides of steak with ¼ cup water and sprinkle with meat tenderizer. Place steak in center of a lightly oiled square of double-thick heavy-duty foil. Cover with ⅓ cup of the mardinade mixture. Seal package and place on medium-hot coals for about 2 hours. Open packagle, remove steak and place on grill over coals for about 30 more minutes. Baste with remaining marinade, turning occasionally. Cook until meat is brown and crusty. Serves 6 to 8.

FRENCH LOAF

1 large loaf French bread
1 pound ground beef
1 egg, beaten
1 cup Cheddar cheese, grated
½ cup chopped onion

½ cup sliced stuffed green
  olives
1 8-ounce can tomato sauce
1 teaspoon salt
¼ teaspoon pepper

Cut a slice across the top of the bread, lengthwise, about ½ inch wide. Scoop out bread from crust, leaving a shell, and save 1 cup of bread crumbs. Combine bread crumbs with remaining ingredients. Blend well and place mixture in center of bread shell. Wrap and seal in large lightly oiled square of heavy-duty foil and place package on medium-hot coals for about 1½ hours. Makes 4 to 6 servings.

Here are several recipes that junior outdoor chefs can master, under the guidance of the senior chef, of course.

FOIL BURGERS

1 pound ground beef
salt and pepper
4 slices of onion

4 potatoes, sliced thin
4 tablespoons butter or
  margarine

Season beef with salt and pepper and shape into 4 patties. Place each patty on a lightly oiled square of heavy-duty foil. Top each with an onion and 1 potato slice. Season with salt and pepper; dot with pat of butter or margarine. Seal package and place on medium-hot coals for about 30 minutes, or until done. Turn package once while cooking. Serves 4.

FOIL SURPRISE

1½ pounds ground beef
1½ teaspoons salt
¼ teaspoon pepper

6 slices Cheddar cheese
6 teaspoons pickle relish
6 hamburger buns

Mix beef with salt and pepper and divide into 12 patties. Place 6 patties on lightly oiled squares of heavy-duty foil. Top each patty with a cheese slice and pickle relish. Cover with another hamburger patty. Seal package and place on medium-hot coals for about 30 minutes, turning once. Serve on buns. Serves 6.

FOIL-BAKED POULTRY

The versatile chicken is lower in calories than most other meats, and high in protein, For a savory treat, cook it over the coals wrapped in heavy-duty aluminum foil.

FOIL BARBECUED CHICKEN

1 3-pound frying chicken,
    cut up
½ cup flour
1 teaspoon salt
dash pepper
1 teaspoon paprika
⅓ cup butter or margarine

SAUCE
1 onion, sliced
1 teaspoon salt
1 tablespoon vinegar
1 tablespoon Worcestershire
    sauce
1 tablespoon sugar
¼ teaspoon pepper
½ cup catsup
¼ cup water

Combine all sauce ingredients in small saucepan and bring to boil. Simmer for about 15 minutes. Coat chicken pieces with flour, salt, pepper, paprika in a paper bag. Place chicken pieces on large lightly oiled squares of heavy-duty foil and top with pats of butter or margarine. Cover with barbecue sauce. Seal package and place on medium-hot coals for about 1 hour, turning occasionally. Serves 6 to 8.

Note: If desired, bottle barbecue sauce can be substituted for convenience.

Master Campfire Chef Mrs. Richard K. Hartman, of Ann Arbor, Michigan, won sixth place in the main dish category of our recent Open Fire Camp Cooking contest with this recipe for a delicious chicken dinner cooked in heavy-duty foil.

CHICKEN BAKE

For individual serving:

½ broiler chicken	1 carrot, pared
salt and pepper	1 potato, sliced
paprika	1 onion, sliced
butter or margarine	2 slices bacon

Season half broiler with salt, pepper and paprika and place skin-side down on large lightly oiled square of heavy-duty foil. Dot with butter or margarine and place vegetables in cavity. Top with bacon. Add additional seasoning if desired. Seal package and place on medium-hot coals for about 1½ hours, turning occasionally. During the last 15 minutes of cooking time, poke several holes in the foil so the chicken can brown.

Turkey is an ideal campsite dish because it adapts readily to aluminum foil cooking. Buy young, tender birds and have the butcher quarter or halve them. Then follow this recipe for a succulent taste treat.

BABY TURKEY IN FOIL

2 4- to 5 pound baby turkeys, quartered

1 8-ounce bottle garlic and herb salad dressing
1 cup chicken broth

Marinate turkey pieces in dressing and broth and let stand for about 1 hour. Place each turkey quarter on a large lightly oiled square of heavy-duty foil. Pour 3 to 4 tablespoons of marinade over each quarter. Seal packages and place on medium-hot coals for about 1 hour. Open packages and place opened packages directly over coals and cook for about 30 minutes longer or until golden brown. Brush with remaining marinade during the final cooking time. Serves 8.

Delicately flavored Cornish game hens become elegant campsite fare when they're cooked in foil. Best of all, they're low in calories and surprisingly low in cost.

FOILED BIRDS

6 12-ounce Cornish game hens, whole
1 tablespoon salt
1 teaspoon pepper

SAUCE
1 cup butter or margarine
1 tablespoon liquid gravy seasoning
1 tablespoon grated lemon rind

Season cavity of each game hen with salt and pepper. Combine sauce ingredients in saucepan and heat. Place each game hen on a large lightly oiled square of heavy-duty foil and cover with sauce. Seal package and place on medium-hot coals for about 45 minutes. Open packages and place opened packages directly over coals for about 15 minutes longer, or until golden brown. Turn frequently and brush with remaining sauce. Serves 6.

If desired, stuff each bird with your favorite bread stuffing, and then cook as above.

FISH IN FOIL

This recipe for barbecued fish is one of our favorites. It was given to us by a friendly campground owner who just happens to manage a trout farm!

FISHERMEN'S STEW

2 fresh trout, 2-3 pounds, cleaned	1 medium onion, sliced
salt and pepper	2 potatoes, sliced
	bottle barbecue sauce

Place the fish on lightly oiled squares of heavy-duty foil. Season with salt and pepper. Fill each body cavity with onion and potato slices. Cover fish with barbecue sauce. Seal package and place on medium-hot coals for about 15 minutes, turning once. Serves 4 to 5.

FOIL-BAKED BREAD

Foiled-baked bread is a delicious accompaniment to a hearty campsite meal.

HERB DINNER BREAD

1 loaf French bread
½ cup softened butter or
  margarine

1 teaspoon marjoram

Combine butter or margarine with marjoram. Make 16 slices into French bread, cutting to within ½ inch of bottom. Brush cut surfaces with butter–marjoram mixture. Wrap in heavy-duty aluminum foil, leaving foil partially open at top. Place on medium-hot coals for about 10 minutes, or until hot.

BBQ BREAD

1 loaf French bread
½ cup softened butter or
  margarine

2 teaspoons garlic salad
  dressing mix

Combine butter or margarine with garlic mix. Make 16 slices into French bread, cutting to within ½ inch of bottom. Brush cut surfaces with butter–garlic mixture. Wrap in heavy-duty foil, place on grill, and heat for about 10 minutes.

Foiled Campfire Treats

Nothing compares with the fragrance and the flavor of fruit freshly plucked from a vine or a tree. Eaten raw—or cooked in foil on the coals—fruit makes an ideal campsite dessert.

ROAST BANANAS

bananas   lemon juice
brown sugar

Peel bananas and place each one on a square of heavy-duty foil. Sprinkle each with 1 tablespoon brown sugar and a little lemon juice. Seal package and place on medium-hot coals for about 15 minutes.

FOIL PEACHES

peaches   brown sugar
melted butter   butter or margarine

Peel, halve and stone fresh peaches. Brush with melted butter and place each half on a square of heavy-duty foil. Sprinkle brown sugar into each cavity and dot with additional butter or margarine. Seal package and place on medium-hot coals for about 5 minutes.

RAISIN AND NUT PEARS

pears
melted butter
raisins

chopped nuts
butter or margarine

Peel, halve and stone pears. Brush with melted butter and place on squares of heavy-duty aluminum foil. Fill centers with raisins and chopped nuts; dot with butter or margarine. Seal package and place on medium-hot coals for 10 minutes.

FOILED STRAWBERRIES

1 quart fresh strawberries   ¾ cup granulated sugar

Wash berries, remove hulls and slice in bowl. Sprinkle with sugar, blending well. Place individual servings on squares of heavy-duty foil. Seal package and place on medium-hot coals for about 10 minutes.

MINCEMEAT ORANGES

6 navel oranges   ⅓ cup orange juice
1½ cups canned mincemeat

Peel each orange, leaving about ½ inch of peel around the base. Open orange, keeping sections attached at the base. Place ¼ cup mincemeat into the center of each orange and place orange on square of heavy-duty foil. Add 1 tablespoon orange juice to each orange. Seal packages and place on medium-hot coals for about 45 minutes. Do not turn. Open foil, bake 5 minutes uncovered. Serves 6.

An apple a day won't keep the doctor away, but if you eat one with its jacket on you'll be adding to your daily quota of Vitamin C. The peel of an apple contains three to five times as much of this vitamin as the flesh.

FOIL-ROASTED APPLES

6 medium apples
raisins
¼ cup brown sugar

½ teaspoon cinnamon
2 tablespoons butter or
   margarine

Core apples and scoop out some of the flesh. Fill each cavity with 1 teaspoon of raisins. Top with a mixture of sugar and cinnamon; dot with butter or margarine. Place each prepared apple on a large square of heavy-duty foil. Seal packages and place on medium-hot coals for about 45 minutes, or until apples are tender.

Variations

Other ingredients, such as canned mincemeat, chopped nuts, cloves or marshmallows can also be added to the center of each apple.

Some of the most fun we've had camping has been in the fall when the air is crisp and the leaves are blazing with color. That's the time of year to roast chestnuts over the coals of your campfire.

FOIL-ROASTED CHESTNUTS

3 dozen chestnuts
warm water

2 tablespoons salt
disposable foil pan

Cover chestnuts with water and let stand for about 30 minutes; drain. With a paring knife, make a crisscross cut in the top of each nut. Place a single layer of nuts in the bottom of a foil pan and sprinkle with salt. Cover pan with a square of aluminum foil. Cook on medium-hot coals for about 15 minutes. Remove pan from coals, open and stir chestnuts. Reseal and place again over coals for another 15 minutes, or until tender.

6
Reflector Oven Cooking

THANKSGIVING VISITORS to Old Sturbridge Village at Sturbridge, Massachusetts meet history face to face when they watch village farm wives, dressed in authentic costumes, re-create a typical New England holiday feast of 150 years ago. Highlight of the banquet, which takes place annually in the kitchen of the restored Pliny Freeman Farm, is a huge turkey roasting in an antique tin reflector oven placed beside the open hearth.

Reflector ovens were common kitchen appliances 150 years ago when cooking depended on the ago-old open hearth and the wood-fueled oven. By 1830, however, the more efficient cast-iron range nosed its way into the household and caused the gradual demise of the kitchen fireplace and open-fire cooking.

Once the kitchen became mechanized, only pioneers and outdoorsmen carried on the timeless art of open-fire cookery, and their tin baking ovens were the forerunners of our modern-day camper reflector oven—a handy piece of camp cooking gear our family couldn't do without.

The basic principle of a reflector oven is that it utilizes indirect heat from a fire to bake food. The heat from the flames is reflected onto the slanted faces of the oven, which reflect the heat onto the baking shelf. The degree of heat on the shelf is regulated by moving the oven closer to or farther away from the fire.

Our family was introduced to the joys of reflector oven cooking several years ago when a camping friend invited us to his campsite for dinner. After gorging ourselves on succulent trout baked in his reflector oven, we wasted no time buying an oven of our own. The one we selected was a one-piece aluminum model that folds into a compact package for easy storing in our trailer.

We should mention that if you're an avid "do-it-yourselfer," you can improvise your own reflector oven using cookie sheets or aluminum foil. Our commercial oven was so inexpensive, and is so convenient to use, however, that making one seems hardly worth the effort.

Baking with a reflector oven is basically the same as baking with a conventional oven, but it has two bonuses. It's nice to smell the delicious aroma of food cooking outdoors, and it's fun to watch the biscuits rise and the cakes turn a delicate golden-brown right before your eyes.

Our experiences with reflector oven cooking have taught us a few simple but effective tricks that lead to better outdoor baking.

We've learned, for instance, that the kind of campfire we build does make a difference in the efficiency of our oven. When recipes require an hour or more cooking time, we build a hardwood fire (see Chapter 4 . . . Fire Building, page 21) which burns for a long period of time with a steady, even flame.

When we bake biscuits, quick breads or any of the packaged mixes that requires a 10- to 20-minute cooking time, we build a softwood fire (see page 22) which burns with a hot flame for a relatively short period of time. A softwood fire produces an ash which occasionally drifts onto the baking shelf, but it's harmless and can easily be blown away.

We've also learned that no matter what kind of fire we build, frequent stoking is necessary to keep our fire burning with a high flame.

As with a conventional oven, a reflector oven should be preheated before placing food on the baking shelf. We've heard of several methods of judging when the baking shelf is hot enough for cooking. We find the simplest way is to place our hand inside the oven and use common sense. If it feels hot, the oven is ready. Once the oven is hot, however, don't move it without using asbestos gloves on both hands.

To maintain the efficiency of our reflector oven we wash it after three or four uses in hot sudsy water and remove the soot that collects on the surface with a soap-filled steel wool pad. This restores the bright reflective finish of the aluminum.

Like most beginners, when we first used our reflector oven we tested our outdoor cooking skills using prepared mixes. Once we discovered how good they tasted cooked with reflected heat, we began baking more complicated quick breads and desserts and then finally graduated to meat and fish dishes. Now we bake anything that fits on our baking shelf.

To encourage potential reflector oven chefs, we've included in this chapter recipes that are simple to prepare and bake. They're just a sample of the many dishes that can be baked with a reflector oven.

Before you prepare any of the recipes, however, be sure your baking pan fits on the oven shelf. We use a 9-x-7-inch aluminum pan that bakes a variety of dishes from corn bread to meat loaf.

At least once during baking, turn your pan around, front to back, so that the food will bake evenly on both sides. If baking biscuits, turn them over with tongs.

Of necessity, cooking times given with the recipes are approximate and vary depending on the heat of your fire. By touching cakes and muffins lightly with your fingertip you'll be able to tell whether they're done. If the dent made by your fingertip springs back, lift the pan off the shelf with hot pads. And remember, if you're a conscientious fire watcher and maintain a consistently high flame, you'll be able to bake most dishes at the normal baking rate of your galley oven.

Now that you know how easy reflector oven baking is, come join us while we prepare some of our family's favorite dishes. Better yet, why not get a reflector oven of your own and bake your family's favorite foods.

Reflector Oven-Baked Breakfast Cakes, Breads and Muffins

It's hard to resist the tantalizing aroma of fresh-baked goods, especially when they're served with morning coffee. To make these quick breads and muffins, rekindle the evening campfire and heat up your reflector oven. Serve your breakfast sweets with fresh-perked coffee and you'll be all set for an invigorating morning hike.

SPEEDY COFFEECAKE

1 package muffin mix
2 tablespoons butter or margarine

¼ cup brown sugar
1 medium-size can sliced pears

Melt butter or margarine in a 9-inch-square pan. Sprinkle with brown sugar, and arrange pear slices over mixture. Prepare muffin mix as per directions on package. Place batter over pears. Place baking pan on reflector oven shelf and bake for about 20 to 30 minutes.

BREAKFAST CAKE

1⅓ cups biscuit mix
⅔ cup sugar
1 egg
¾ cup milk

TOPPING:
2 tablespoons butter or margarine
½ cup brown sugar
¾ cup chopped nuts

Combine biscuit mix, sugar, egg and milk, blending well.

Pour batter into lightly greased 9-inch pan. Bake on reflector oven shelf for about 20 minutes, or until brown. Melt butter or margarine, add brown sugar and nuts and brush on top of cake. Return to oven to brown.

CINNAMON CAKE

½ cup sugar
½ cup flour
1 tablespoon baking powder
½ teaspoon salt
1 egg

½ cup milk
4 tablespoons melted butter
  or margarine
sugar and cinnamon

Mix sugar, flour, baking powder and salt. Add egg, milk and melted butter or margarine. Blend well. Place batter in a greased 9-inch pan. Sprinkle top with sugar and cinnamon mixture. Bake on reflector oven shelf for about 15 minutes.

QUICK DATE BREAD

1 package date bread mix
1 egg
water
½ cup butter or margarine

½ cup brown sugar
½ teaspoon vanilla
½ cup chopped nuts

Prepare date bread mix with egg and water as per directions on package. Melt butter or margarine in small pan, stir in sugar and vanilla. Sprinkle nuts into a lightly greased baking pan. Pour sugar–butter mixture over nuts. Spoon date bread batter over top. Place on reflector oven shelf and bake for 30 to 40 minutes.

NUTTY BREAD

2 cups flour
¾ cup sugar
3 teaspoons baking powder
1 teaspoon salt
½ teaspoon cinnamon

1 egg, beaten
1 cup applesauce
2 tablespoons melted butter or
  margarine
1 cup chopped nuts

Sift dry ingredients together into mixing bowl. Combine egg, applesauce and melted butter or margarine and add to dry ingredients, blending well. Add chopped nuts. Spread batter in lightly greased baking pan and place on reflector oven shelf. Bake for about 40 minutes.

REFLECTOR MUFFINS

2 cups flour
2 tablespoons sugar
3 teaspoons baking powder
½ teaspoon salt

1 cup milk
1 egg
2 tablespoons oil
cooked fruit, jelly or cheese

Lightly grease muffin cups. Sift flour, sugar, baking powder and salt together. Mix milk, egg and cooking oil together in another bowl, blending well. Pour liquid mixture into dry mixture; stir. Batter will be lumpy. Spoon butter into muffin cups and place a piece of cooked fruit, a spoon of jelly or a cheese cube in center of the batter. Bake on reflector oven shelf until muffins are brown, or about 20 minutes.

BLUEBERRY MUFFINS

2 cups biscuit mix
¼ cup sugar for batter

½ teaspoon cinnamon
1 egg, unbeaten

1 cup sour cream (or sour half   1 cup fresh blueberries
   and half)   sugar for sprinkling

Lightly grease muffin cups. In mixing bowl, combine biscuit mix, ¼ cup sugar and cinnamon; blend well. In another bowl, blend egg with cream and stir into dry mixture. Beat with fork until well blended. Gently fold in blueberries. Spoon batter into muffin cups, sprinkle each with sugar. Bake on reflector oven shelf until muffins are brown, or about 20 minutes.

Tender biscuits broken open with a fork and spread lavishly with butter make delectable campsite dining. Here's one of our favorite biscuit recipes. Other biscuit recipes suited to reflector oven cooking may be found in the chapter on Dutch Oven Cooking.

CREAM OF TARTAR BISCUITS

3 cups flour   1 teaspoon salt
2 teaspoons cream of tartar   ⅓ cup shortening
1 teaspoon baking soda   1¾ cups milk

Sift dry ingredients together and cut in shortening. Blend until mixture is crumbly. Add milk and mix, blending until all the flour is moistened. Pat dough to about ½ inch thick and cut into rounds. Place biscuits on greased baking pan, and place pan on reflector oven shelf. Bake for about 20 minutes, or until golden brown.

No camp cookbook would be complete without a recipe for corn bread, so here it is.

REFLECTOR OVEN CORN BREAD

1 cup cornmeal	4 tablespoons sugar
1 cup all-purpose flour	1 cup milk
3 teaspoons baking powder	1 egg
½ teaspoon salt	¼ cup shortening

Blend dry ingredients together. Add milk and egg and stir until smooth. Add shortening and blend. Pour into greased baking pan and place on reflector oven shelf. Bake for about 20 minutes, or until top is brown.

REFLECTOR OVEN-BAKED MEALS

After a day of fresh air and lots of outdoor activity, most campers are ready for a hearty evening meal. Build up your campfire, heat your reflector oven and try this recipe for a flavorful Sausage Corn Bread supper. The recipe comes from Master Campfire Chef Mrs. Virginia W. Welch of Rochester, New York and it won fourth prize in the main dish category of Woodall's 1969 Open Fire Camp Cooking contest.

SAUSAGE CORN BREAD SUPPER

1 box brown-and-serve sausage	1 box corn muffin mix
6 to 8 apple rings	1 large jar applesauce

Brown sausage on all sides in skillet over hot coals. Core, pare and slice apples into rings and place rings in bottom of baking pan. Cover apples with browned sausage. Prepare corn muffin mix according to directions on package, and pour batter over sausage and apples. Place on reflector oven shelf and bake for 20 to 25 minutes.

Heat applesauce in pan. When muffin–sausage mixture is baked, remove from fire and invert on serving dish. Top with hot applesauce.

For another substantial evening meal bake a flavorful ham loaf.

PINEAPPLE HAM

butter	1 pound ground ham
brown sugar	½ cup bread crumbs
4 slices canned pineapple,	½ cup milk
drained	2 eggs, beaten

Lightly butter baking pan and sprinkle bottom with brown sugar. Place pineapple slices on top of sugar. For eye appeal, add a cherry in the center of each slice of pineapple. Mix ground ham with bread crumbs, milk and eggs and spread over pineapple. Place on reflector oven shelf and bake for about 40 minutes, or until ham is done. Remove from oven and invert on serving dish. Serves 4.

Probably every campfire chef has a file crammed full of ground beef recipes, and we're no exception. Here are two ground beef recipes that make superb eating when baked in a reflector oven.

MEAT LOAF ITALIANO

2 pounds ground beef
1 10½-ounce can condensed
   tomato soup
¼ can water
½ teaspoon oregano
1 clove garlic, minced
1 cup bread crumbs

¼ cup chopped onion
2 tablespoons chopped parsley
1 egg, beaten
1 teaspoon salt
dash pepper
2 slices cheese (processed or
   Mozzarella)

Blend soup, water, oregano and minced garlic. In bowl, combine ¼ cup of soup mixture with bread crumbs, onion, parsley, egg, salt and pepper. Mix thoroughly with ground beef and shape into loaf. Place in baking pan and place pan on reflector oven shelf. Bakes for 1½ hours, or until meat is done. Remove from oven, spoon off fat. Pour remaining soup over meat, top with cheese and return to baking shelf. Bake until cheese is melted. Serves 6 to 8.

MUSHROOM MEAT LOAF

1½ pounds ground beef
1 10½-ounce can condensed
   golden mushroom soup
1 cup bread crumbs
¼ cup chopped onion
1 egg

½ teaspoon salt
dash pepper
2 cups instant mashed potatoes
¼ cup water
1–2 tablespoons drippings

Mix ground beef with ½ cup soup, bread crumbs, onion, egg, salt and pepper. Shape into loaf and place in baking pan. Place pan on reflector oven shelf and bake for about 1 hour, or until meat is done. Prepare instant mashed potatoes according to directions on package. Place prepared potatoes on top of meat loaf. Return to oven and bake about 15 minutes longer. Blend remaining soup with water and drippings. Heat on camp stove and serve with loaf.

Serves 6 to 8.

Wiener Wurstchen, *the sausages that are the forerunners of the American wiener, were first sold by concessionaires in a lively amusement park in Vienna, Austria, in the eighteenth century. Now these reddish sausages of beef and pork have become a typically American dish, relished at the ball park, the beach and the campsite.*

Remember that wieners, or frankfurters, are thoroughly cooked when you buy them and only need heating before serving. And they taste extra good when baked in a reflector oven.

BEANS AND FRANKS

1 1-pound can pork and beans
6 frankfurters, cut into 1-inch
　slices
3 tablespoons brown sugar
3 tablespoons molasses
¼ cup catsup

1 tablespoon prepared mustard
½ cup canned pineapple
　chunks, drained
½ cup sliced canned peaches,
　drained

Combine all the above ingredients together and place in baking pan. Place pan on reflector oven shelf and bake for 30 or 40 minutes.

Serves 6.

FRANKWICHES

1 pound frankfurters, cut into 1-inch slices	¼ cup catsup
2 tablespoons mustard	2 cups biscuit mix
	water

Mix frankfurter slices with mustard and catsup. Mix biscuit mix with a small amount of water to form dough. Pat dough flat to ¼-inch thickness and cut into small squares. Divide meat mixture and place small amount on each square. Cover with another biscuit square to make sandwich. Place sandwiches in pan on reflector oven shelf and bake for 15 to 20 minutes, or until biscuit dough is brown. Serves 4 to 6.

SCALLOPS AND FRANKS

½ pound frankfurters, sliced   1 package scalloped potatoes

Mix frankfurter slices with package of scalloped potatoes. Cook according to package directions, placing baking dish on reflector oven shelf. Serves 4.

CHIPPER FRANKS

1 pound frankfurters, split lengthwise	½ cup crushed corn chips
1 8-ounce can tomato sauce with mushrooms	½ medium onion, chopped
1 cup shredded Cheddar cheese	1 teaspoon Worcestershire sauce

Place split franks in baking dish. Combine one half of the tomato sauce with remaining ingredients and fill franks with mixture. Pour remaining sauce over franks. Place baking pan on reflector oven shelf and cook for about 20 to 30 minutes. Serves 4 to 6.

BUCKING BRONCOS

6 frankfurters   1 package corn bread mix

Prepare corn bread mix according to directions on package. Place franks in baking pan, cover with corn bread batter. Place baking pan on reflector oven shelf and cook until golden brown, about 20 minutes. Serves 6.

REFLECTOR OVEN-BAKED FISH

If the fish you caught are "keepers," take a snapshot for posterity, take them off your stringer and clean them as soon as possible. Then bake your catch in the preheated reflector oven.

BAKED FISH

Clean fish, and, if small, cook whole. Place cleaned fish in shallow, lightly greased baking pan. Season with salt and pepper. Cover with thin slices of bacon. Place baking pan on reflector oven shelf and cook for about 45 minutes, or until fish is flaky.

FISH BAKED IN MILK

Prepare fish for baking. Place in shallow, lightly greased baking pan. Season with salt and pepper. Pour 1 cup milk over fish and cook as for baked fish.

REFLECTOR OVEN-BAKED DESSERTS

A good way to increase your protein intake for the day is to serve a dessert that includes cheese or eggs. Here's a recipe with cheese as one of the principal ingredients.

CHEESE APPLES

6 cups apple slices
1 tablespoon lemon juice
1 cup sugar
¼ teaspoon cinnamon
½ cup unsifted flour
¼ teaspoon salt
¼ cup butter or margarine
⅔ cup Cheddar cheese, finely shredded

Place apple slices in lightly greased baking pan. Sprinkle with lemon juice and ¼ cup of the sugar. Mix cinnamon, flour, salt and remaining sugar together. Mix in butter or margarine and stir until mixture is crumbly. Stir in cheese. Spread mixture over apples, place baking pan on reflector oven shelf and cook for about 45 minutes, or until apples are tender.

Here's a recipe that's especially good in the fall, when apples are plentiful.

APPLE CRISP

4–5 large apples, pared and
   sliced
1 cup brown sugar

1 cup flour
½ cup butter or margarine

Place apple slices in greased baking pan. Mix sugar and flour together, add butter or margarine and stir until the mixture is crumbly. Sprinkle mixture over apples. Place pan on reflector oven shelf and bake for about 30 minutes, or until apples are tender.

Fruit cobblers are easy dishes to prepare when you're away on a camping vacation. And we think they taste better when cooked outdoors in a reflector oven.

CHERRY COBBLER

1 can (1 pound, 5 ounces)
   prepared cherry pie filling
¼ cup water
1 tablespoon butter or
   margarine
½ teaspoon cinnamon

1½ cups sweet cream
   pancake mix
2 tablespoons sugar
¼ cup shortening
½ cup milk

Combine pie filling, water, butter or margarine and cinnamon in large saucepan and heat until bubbly. Spoon into a baking pan. Combine pancake mix and sugar, add shortening and mix until crumbly. Add milk. Stir until well blended, and drop batter by spoonfuls on top of cherry mixture. Place pan on reflector oven shelf and bake for about 20 minutes, or until brown.

COBBLER PIE

1 cup flour
1 cup sugar
1½ teaspoons baking powder
¼ teaspoon salt
1 teaspoon cinnamon

¾ cup sweet milk
1 No. 303 can blueberry pie
  filling
butter

Sift dry ingredients together. Add milk and blend well. Pour batter into lightly greased baking pan. Then pour blueberry filling over batter and dot with butter. Place pan on reflector oven shelf and bake for about 45 minutes, or until brown.

OZARK COBBLER

1 egg, beaten
1 cup sugar
2 tablespoons flour
1 teaspoon baking powder

dash salt
1 cup chopped apples
½ cup chopped nuts

Combine egg and sugar; beat until creamy. Add flour, baking powder and salt to egg mixture, blending well. Fold in apples and nuts. Spread batter in greased baking pan, place pan on reflector oven shelf and cook for about 30 minutes, or until brown and crusty.

When you're sitting around an evening campfire, enjoying friendly conversation, set up the reflector oven and satisfy your sweet tooth with an easily prepared treat.

DESSERT TIDBIT

1 tube refrigerated baking
   powder biscuits
butter

plum jam
nutmeg
chopped nuts

Open tube and flatten biscuits on ungreased baking pan. Spread each biscuit with butter and top with jam. Sprinkle nutmeg over jam, and add spoonful of chopped nuts. Place on reflector oven shelf and bake for about 10 minutes, or until biscuits are brown.

BANANA DELIGHT

8 ripe bananas
juice of two oranges
½ cup brown sugar

1 cup shredded coconut
½ cup bread crumbs

Peel bananas and cut in halves. Arrange halves in greased baking pan. Mix juice with sugar and pour over bananas. Mix coconut with bread crumbs and sprinkle over mixture. Place pan on reflector oven shelf and bake for about 10 minutes, or until coconut is brown.

7
Dutch Oven Cooking

THREE-LEGGED CAMPER Dutch ovens claim an ancient heritage and actually stem from the same family tree that earlier produced the large iron cauldrons used by medieval cooks in the 13th century and the small three-legged cooking pots with lids which were popular with Renaissance chefs in the 16th century. More recent relatives include the trail ovens used by American colonists as they moved westward across our country in the 18th and 19th centuries.

The Dutch oven is a versatile cooking pot that can substitute for a host of outdoor cooking utensils. With its snug-fitting lid in place, and heated with coals from a wood or charcoal fire, it becomes an oven where food can be baked, braised, stewed or roasted. With the lid removed, the oven becomes a kettle for boiling, deep-fat frying or for heating food quickly over a fire. Even the oven lid doubles in service and can be converted into a frying pan.

A true camper Dutch oven is easily identified by its legs which extend below the oven and permit it to sit over hot coals and by its flat lid which has a vertical lip around the outside edge to retain the hot coals which are placed on top.

There are several types of Dutch ovens available and each performs equally well. Our family owns a round 10-inch cast-iron oven and a round 12-inch cast-aluminum oven. Also on the market is a rectangular oven constructed of aluminum.

Our aluminum oven is my favorite because it's lightweight, rustproof and required no breaking in. In addition, it can be cleaned with any accepted utensil cleanser.

Our aluminum oven heats rapidly and for normal cooking requires 10 to 12 coals underneath and 15 to 18 coals on the lid. Experience has taught us never to try speeding up cooking time by using an excessive amount of coals since this damages the aluminum and causes the food to burn.

We also prepare many meals with our cast-iron oven. It's somewhat heavier than the aluminum one and takes longer to heat, but we like it because it heats evenly and stays hot for a long time.

Like most cast-iron cookware, our oven came preseasoned, which meant there was no antirust lacquer for us to remove. Before using it for the first time we applied a light coating of unsalted shortening inside the oven and the lid and heated them in our kitchen oven. After each use we wash the oven and lid in hot soapy water, and after drying them we again grease the inside and the lid with unsalted shortening. The next time we use the oven we wipe these surfaces with a paper towel.

Our cast-iron oven requires more cooking coals than our aluminum one, but the ratio of coals on top to coals underneath remains the same. We place 15 to 17 coals below the oven and 20 to 24 coals on the lid.

To keep our cast-iron oven from "sweating" when not in use, we remove the lid and store the oven upside down on a rack, with the lid right-side up on top of the legs. We store our aluminum oven upright with the lid in place.

Since firewood isn't always available, when we want hot cooking coals for either oven we use charcoal and a metal charcoal lighter. If a lighter isn't handy we start the briquettes with fluid and allow 20 to 30 minutes for them to heat properly before placing them around the oven. When we're able to build a campfire we try to burn woods that produce lots of hot coals.

Hickory, white ash, white oak, canoe birch and black locust all burn evenly and provide a good bed of coals. Beech, dogwood and sugar maple are also excellent firewoods for cooking. (See Chapter 4 . . . Fire Building)

To demonstrate the many talents of the camper Dutch oven, we've included a variety of recipes in this chapter—dishes that range from stews and barbecues to baked goods and desserts. Cooking time given for each recipe is approximate, however, since the degree of heat inside a Dutch oven depends on the kind of oven used and on the hotness of the cooking coals.

It's best not to guess at cooking time, and we suggest you check the food from time to time by removing the oven lid with hot-pot tongs. By clamping the tongs onto the vertical lip of the lid, you can raise the lid and move it to one side without disturbing the cooking coals.

Dutch ovens are fun to use, and we find them especially convenient in hot weather when we want to prepare a large cut of meat without heating up our rig by turning on our galley oven.

If your family isn't acquainted with an authentic camper Dutch oven, we suggest you make friends with one right away. Use your oven to prepare leisurely campsite meals and then settle back and enjoy some of the most delectable dishes you've ever eaten.

MEAT IN A DUTCH OVEN

Traditionally, meat stew is made by browning seasoned, floured meat in a small amount of fat, covering it with hot water or stock and then cooking it slowly in a covered kettle for a long period of time.

A camper Dutch oven is an ideal utensil for making stews because it remains hot for hours without scorching the food and because its tight-fitting lid permits a stew to slow simmer with no loss of flavor.

The following recipe for an old-fashioned bean and bacon stew was brought to this country by pioneers from Germany.

BEAN AND BACON STEW

1 pound dried white kidney beans
1 pound smoked bacon, unsliced and cut into 1-inch cubes
3 tablespoons butter or margarine

4 large half-ripe pears, peeled, cored and cubed
1 onion, sliced
1 teaspoon salt
½ teaspoon pepper

Follow directions on bean package and either soak beans overnight or parboil. Preheat Dutch oven over coals. Melt butter or margarine in oven and brown cubed bacon in hot fat. Drain beans and add to bacon along with pears, onion, seasonings and enough water to cover. Place lid on oven and cover with hot coals. Cook for about 1 hour, or until beans are tender. Serves 6.

Lamb stew is a traditional dish that's been around for centuries. Many lamb stew recipes call for the addition of dill, but since we don't carry that ancient spice while trailering, we make our lamb stew in a Dutch oven where the vegetables and meat blend in a savory one-dish meal.

the food and because its tight-fitting lid permits a stew to slow simmer with no loss of flavor.

The following recipe for an old-fashioned bean and bacon stew was brought to this country by pioneers from Germany.

BEAN AND BACON STEW

1 pound dried white kidney beans

1 pound smoked bacon, unsliced and cut into 1-inch cubes

3 tablespoons butter or margarine

4 large half-ripe pears, peeled, cored and cubed

1 onion, sliced

1 teaspoon salt

½ teaspoon pepper

Follow directions on bean package and either soak beans overnight or parboil. Preheat Dutch oven over coals. Melt butter or margarine in oven and brown cubed bacon in hot fat. Drain beans and add to bacon along with pears, onion, seasonings and enough water to cover. Place lid on oven and cover with hot coals. Cook for about 1 hour, or until beans are tender. Serves 6.

Lamb stew is a traditional dish that's been around for centuries. Many lamb stew recipes call for the addition of dill, but since we don't carry that ancient spice while trailering, we make our lamb stew in a Dutch oven where the vegetables and meat blend in a savory one-dish meal.

SETTLER'S STEW

3 pounds beef for stew
6 tablespoons salad oil
1 cup chopped onion
1 cup chopped green pepper
1 cup sliced celery
½ cup water
1 10½-ounce can condensed
  beef broth
1 8-ounce can tomato sauce
2 tablespoons chopped parsley
1 clove garlic, finely chopped
1 tablespoon salt
¼ teaspoon pepper
1 bay leaf
6 potatoes, pared and halved
6 carrots, pared and quartered
6 small white onions
1–2 tablespoons flour
2 tablespoons water
1 tomato, cut in wedges

Preheat Dutch oven over coals. Brown beef in oil, add onion, green pepper and celery and sauté until tender. Add ½ cup water, beef broth, tomato sauce, parsley, garlic, salt, pepper and bay leaf. Place lid on oven and cover with hot coals. Cook for about 1¼ hours. Remove lid, add potatoes, carrots and onions. Cover and cook for about 1 more hour. Remove lid, skim off fat. Mix flour with 2 tablespoons water and stir into liquid. Cook 5 more minutes until mixture thickens slightly. Arrange tomato wedges skinside up on top and simmer covered for about 10 minutes more. Serves 4 to 6.

For an interesting combination of flavors, try beef stew with pork sausage.

TWO-POUND HOT POT

2 pounds beef round
2 pounds pork sausage
2 pounds potatoes, pared
2 pounds onions, peeled

2 pounds apples	flour
2 pounds tomatoes	water
salt, pepper	

Cut beef, pork sausage, pared potatoes, peeled onions, apples and tomatoes into bite-size pieces. Roll in seasoned flour or shake in a bag containing seasoned flour. Place all ingredients in cold Dutch oven in layers and add water, covering all but the next to last layer. Place lid on oven and cover with hot coals. Cook for about 1 hour. Remove lid, stir and re-cover. Cook for about 1½ hours more. Serves 6 to 8.

The delightful aroma of Mulligan Stew simmering in a country kitchen evokes many pleasant memories. Yet we think Mulligan himself would agree stew never tasted better than it does when cooked outdoors in a Dutch oven.

MULLIGAN STEW

1½ pounds round steak, cubed	1 teaspoon Worcestershire
2 tablespoons shortening	sauce
flour	1½ cups water
salt and pepper	4 onions, diced
½ teaspoon allspice	4 to 5 potatoes, pared and
1 teaspoon sugar	sliced
1 teaspoon lemon juice	3 carrots, sliced
2 cups tomato juice	¾ cup chopped celery

Preheat Dutch oven over coals. Melt shortening. Flour meat and brown in hot fat. Add seasonings, sugar, juices, Worcestershire sauce and water. Place lid on oven and cover with hot coals. Cook for about 1½ hours. Remove lid, add vegetables, cover and cook for about 1 hour more, or until vegetables are tender. Serves 4 to 6.

The camper Dutch oven not only creates delicious, flavorsome stews, but it also excels at braising, roasting and pot roasting. Here's a recipe for a basic pot roast that can be enhanced by adding your own choice of vegetables.

BASIC POT ROAST

3 to 4 pound beef pot roast
3 tablespoons fat
2 teaspoons salt
¼ teaspoon pepper

1 onion, sliced
½ cup water
stew vegetables (optional)

Preheat Dutch oven over coals. Add fat and brown meat on all sides. Season with salt and pepper. Add onion and water. Place lid on oven and cover with hot coals. Cook for about 2½ hours. Vegetables may be added during the last hour of cooking time. Serves 6 to 8.

If you prefer a spicy pot roast try this recipe for Barbecued Pot Roast.

BARBECUED POT ROAST

3-pound beef pot roast
2 teaspoons salt
¼ teaspoon pepper

3 tablespoons fat
½ cup water
1 8-ounce can tomato sauce

3 onions, sliced
1 clove garlic, chopped
2 tablespoons brown sugar
½ teaspoon dry mustard
¼ cup lemon juice

¼ cup catsup
¼ cup vinegar
1 tablespoon Worcestershire
  sauce
flour

Preheat Dutch oven over hot coals. Season meat with salt and pepper. Heat fat in oven and brown meat. Add water, tomato sauce, onions and garlic. Place lid on oven and cover with hot coals. Cook for about 1½ hours. Remove lid and add remaining ingredients. Cover and cook for about 1 hour more, or until meat is tender. Remove lid, take out meat and set aside. Skim fat from liquid. Make paste with flour and water, blend into liquid and cook until thickened. Pour gravy over meat and serve hot. Serves 6 to 8.

Serving a crowd is easy if you give them tangy barbecue beef sandwiches made from a rump roast braised in your Dutch oven.

BEEF BARBECUE

4 pound boned rump roast
3 tablespoons oil
1 onion, chopped
salt and pepper
1 tablespoon sugar
1 teaspoon dry mustard
1 teaspoon salt
1 teaspoon paprika

½ cup catsup
½ cup water
¼ cup vinegar
1 tablespoon Worcestershire
  sauce
2 drops Tabasco sauce
2 tablespoons oil (for Dutch
  oven)

Preheat Dutch oven over coals. In a large skillet, heat 3 tablespoons oil. Sauté onion in hot oil, add remaining ingredients except meat and salt and pepper and simmer on camp stove for about 10 minutes.

Season meat with salt and pepper. Heat 2 tablespoons oil in Dutch oven. Brown meat in hot oil. Pour sauce over meat, place lid on oven and cover with hot coals. Cook for about 4 hours. Remove lid and turn meat every hour. When tender, slice meat thin, serve with sauce on toasted buns. Makes 12 sandwiches.

Thrifty camp chefs can make the most of their meat dollars by braising economical cuts of meat, such as flank steak and short ribs. Cook them to a tender turn in a Dutch oven.

FLANK STEAK

1 flank steak, cubed	⅓ cup catsup
½ cup flour	⅔ cup water
butter or margarine	1 onion, chopped

Preheat Dutch oven over coals. Cut steak into 3-inch cubes and flour. Melt butter or margarine in oven and brown steak in hot fat. Add catsup, water and onion. Place lid on oven and cover with hot coals. Cook for about 1 hour. Remove lid, turn meat and add more water if necessary. Cover and cook for about 30 minutes longer, or until meat is tender. Serves 3 to 4.

DUTCH OVEN SHORT RIBS

3 pounds beef short ribs	½ teaspoon pepper
1½ teaspoons salt	2 onions, sliced

½ teaspoon dry mustard
2 teaspoons lemon juice
2 bay leaves
1½ cups water
¼ cup brown sugar

1 can lima beans (medium size), drained
4 carrots, pared and halved
4 potatoes, pared and halved
flour for gravy

Preheat Dutch oven over coals. Brown short ribs in their own fat. Pour off drippings and season with salt and pepper. Add onions, dry mustard, lemon juice, bay leaves and water. Place lid on oven and cover with hot coals. Cook for about 2 hours. Remove lid, add brown sugar, lima beans, carrots and potatoes. Cover and cook for about 1 more hour, or until vegetables are tender. Discard bay leaves and remove ribs and vegetables to a platter. Thicken cooking liquid with flour. Pour gravy over meat and serve hot. Serves 4 to 6.

Ground beef is not only a popular and inexpensive dish, it's the basis for many delicious campsite meals, as these recipes demonstrate.

FAMILY RICE DINNER

1½ pounds ground beef
1 cup uncooked raw rice (not instant)
¼ cup butter or margarine
½ cup chopped onion
½ cup chopped green pepper
½ cup chopped celery

2 16-ounce cans tomatoes
¼ teaspoon chili powder
2 teaspoons salt
1 teaspoon sugar
½ teaspoon Worcestershire sauce

Preheat Dutch oven over coals. Heat butter or margarine in oven, brown beef and rice in hot fat. Add remaining ingredients and blend well. Place lid on oven and cover with hot coals. Cook for about 1 hour, or until rice is tender. Serves 4 to 6.

CHEROKEE CASSEROLE

1 pound ground beef
2 cups chopped celery
2 onions, chopped
½ cup uncooked raw rice
  (not instant)

1 can cream of chicken soup
1 can mushroom soup
1 can water

Preheat Dutch oven over hot coals. Brown meat, add celery and cook about 5 minutes. Blend in other ingredients. Place lid on oven and cover with hot coals. Cook for about 1 hour, or until rice is tender. Serves 4 to 6.

DUTCH OVEN SPAGHETTI

3 pounds ground beef
4 onions, chopped
1½ pounds mushrooms, sliced
1 cup chopped celery
salt and pepper
1 tablespoon curry powder
  (optional)
2 tablespoons sugar

garlic, clove, minced (or
  garlic salt)
1 28-ounce can tomatoes
1 6-ounce can tomato paste
1 8-ounce package spaghetti,
  cooked
Parmesan cheese, grated
  (optional)

Preheat Dutch oven over hot coals. Brown meat, add onions, mushrooms, celery, seasonings and tomatoes and tomato paste. Blend well. Place lid on oven and cover with hot coals. Cook for about 1 hour. Remove lid, stir, replace lid and continue cooking for about 1 more hour. Serve sauce over cooked, drained spaghetti and sprinkle with grated Parmesan cheese if desired. Serves 8 to 10.

SPAGHETTI AND BONES

2 pounds ground beef
1 pound spareribs, cracked
2 onions, chopped
1 clove garlic, minced
oil
2 teaspoons salt
1 teaspoon pepper

2 bay leaves
2 8-ounce cans tomato sauce
1 12-ounce can tomato paste
4 cups water
1 8-ounce package spaghetti, cooked

Preheat Dutch oven over hot coals. Brown meats with onions and garlic in small amount of oil. Season with salt and pepper, add bay leaves, tomato sauce, tomato paste and water. Place lid on oven and cover with hot coals. Cook for about 1 hour. Remove lid, stir and cover again. Cook for about 1 more hour. Mixture is done when sauce cooks down and meat separates from ribs. Serve over cooked spaghetti. Serves 6 to 8.

Spareribs are juicier and more flavorful when cooked slowly for a long period of time in a Dutch oven. Here are three variations of this popular dish.

ALOHA RIBS

3 to 4 pounds spareribs
3 tablespoons brown sugar
2 tablespoons cornstarch
½ teaspoon salt
¼ cup vinegar

½ cup catsup
1 9-ounce can crushed pineapple
1 tablespoon soy sauce

Preheat Dutch oven over hot coals. In large mixing bowl combine sugar, cornstarch, salt, vinegar, catsup, pineapple and juice and soy sauce. Place mixture in hot oven and cook over coals until mixture is slightly thickened. Arrange ribs in oven, covering with sauce. Place lid on oven and cover with hot coals. Cook for about 1½ hours, or until tender. Serves 6.

BARBECUED RIBS

3 to 4 pounds spareribs
2 onions, sliced
½ cup catsup
1 cup water
½ teaspoon chili powder

1½ tablespoons
  Worcestershire sauce
2 tablespoons vinegar
1 teaspoon salt
1 tablespoon sugar
1 teaspoon dry mustard

Preheat Dutch oven over hot coals. In large mixing bowl, combine all ingredients except meat and onions. Place layer of ribs in hot oven, cover with half the sauce and half the onions. Place second layer of ribs in oven and cover with remaining onions and sauce. Place lid on oven and cover with hot coals. Cook for about 1½ hours, or until tender. Serves 6.

COUNTRY RIBS DE LUXE

4 pounds spareribs
2 cups chopped onion
2 tablespoons paprika
⅓ cup catsup
3 tablespoons vinegar
1 cup water

1½ teaspoon salt
1 cup sour cream (or sour
  half and half))
1 tablespoon flour, mixed with
  water to make a paste

Preheat Dutch oven over hot coals Brown ribs in oven and

remove. Brown onions in oven, add paprika, catsup, vinegar, water and salt. Blend well. Return meat to oven and place in sauce. Place lid on oven and cover with hot coals. Cook for about 1 hour. Remove lid, spoon sauce over ribs, cover and cook for about another hour, or until meat is tender. Remove lid, take out meat and place on platter. Add flour paste to liquid; stir. Add sour cream and blend. Cook liquid over coals until thick. Pour sauce over ribs and serve hot.

Serves 6.

The following recipe for Sweet and Sour Chops comes from Master Campfire Chef Raymond Valenta of Wheaton, Illinois, who won eighth prize with it in the main dish category of Woodall's 1969 Open Fire Camp Cooking contest.

SWEET AND SOUR CHOPS

6 pork chops	1 cup applesauce
1 No. 303 can sauerkraut, drained	salt and pepper
	1 onion, sliced
½ cup brown sugar	2 cups water

Preheat Dutch oven over hot coals. Place chops in hot oven and brown. Remove chops, set aside and drain fat from oven. Place kraut in mixing bowl, add brown sugar and applesauce. Season with salt and pepper, blending well. Place mixture in oven and add browned chops. Place onion and water over chops. Place lid on oven and cover with hot coals. Cook for about 1 hour, until meat is tender.

Serves 6.

Chicken in a Dutch Oven

The delicate flavor, the economy and the wide variety of ways in which chicken can be served makes it a popular dish with campers. The following recipes for chicken make good use of the Dutch oven.

DUTCH ROAST CHICKEN

1 4-pound roasting chicken
salt and pepper
3 tablespoons butter or
  margarine

¼ cup chicken broth, or water
¾ cup cream (or half and half)
1 egg, beaten

Preheat Dutch oven over hot coals. Season chicken with salt and pepper. Fasten body and neck cavities with skewers. Heat butter or margarine in oven and brown chicken on all sides, ending with breast-side up. Add broth (or water) and cream. Place lid on oven and cover lid with hot coals. Cook for about 1 hour, or until tender. Remove chicken and set aside on platter. Skim fat from cooking liquid, stir egg into small amount of cooking liquid and blend with remaining liquid in oven. Cook over coals until thickened. Pour gravy over chicken and serve hot. Serves 4 to 5.

CHICKEN STEW

2 3-pound chickens, cut up
½ cup butter or margarine
2 onions, chopped
2 tablespoons paprika
salt and pepper

1 to 2 cups water or chicken
  broth
2 tablespoons flour
1 cup sour cream

Preheat Dutch oven over hot coals. Heat butter or margarine and brown chicken pieces in hot fat. Remove chicken and set aside. Brown onions in hot fat; add seasonings. Blend well, then return chicken to oven. Add enough water or broth to cover chicken. Place lid on oven and cover lid with hot coals. Cook for about 1 hour, or until chicken is tender.

Blend flour into sour cream. Remove chicken and stir flour mixture into liquid. Cook over coals until thickened. Pour gravy over chicken and serve hot. Serves 6.

Fish in a Dutch Oven

Bouillabaisse by any other name is fish stew, an ancient dish that's a delicacy in the world's best restaurants. The following recipe for camper's fish stew comes from Master Campfire Chef Norman Wolfrom of Erie, Pennsylvania, who won fifth prize with it in Woodall's 1969 Open Fire Camp Cooking contest.

DUTCH OVEN FISH STEW

1 pound bacon cut into
  ¼-inch slices
2–3 pounds fresh fish cut into
  2-inch chunks (leave in
  bones, they add to flavor)
4 onions, sliced

8 potatoes, pared and sliced
water
1 teaspoon salt
¼ teaspoon pepper
dash celery salt
dried red pepper to taste

Preheat Dutch oven over hot coals. Place bacon in oven and cook over hot coals. After bacon is brown, remove and set aside, leaving grease in kettle. Place layers of fish, onions and potatoes in oven, repeating layers until oven is filled to about 2 inches from the top. Add water to cover potatoes. Then add seasonings. Place oven over hot coals without the lid and boil mixture until potatoes and fish are tender, 30 to 45 minutes. (After 10 minutes a foam will develop but do not remove or stir.) Serves 6 to 8.

If the fish didn't give you a nibble, on the way back to camp stop at a market and pick up some halibut. For a unique flavor experience, pot roast the halibut in your Dutch oven.

HALIBUT POT ROAST

3 pounds halibut
1 cup flour
½ cup cooking oil
6 carrots, pared and quartered
6 onions, sliced
2 cups chopped celery

6 potatoes, pared and quartered
1 clove garlic, chopped
salt and pepper
2 cups water
¼ cup flour (for paste)

Preheat Dutch oven over hot coals. Remove skin from fish and bone. Roll in flour. Heat oil in oven and brown fish in hot oil. Place vegetables around fish, season with salt and pepper. Add water, place lid on oven and cover with hot coals. Cook for about 1 hour, or until tender. Remove fish and vegetables and set aside on platter. Thicken cooking liquid with paste made with flour and water, blend well and cook over coals until mixture thickens. Pour sauce over fish and vegetables and serve hot. Serves 6 to 8.

Vegetables and Grain Dishes in a Dutch Oven

In some countries, rice is considered to be the perfect food. In our country it's often used as a delicious accompaniment to meat dishes. The following recipe for Scout Rice came from Master Campfire Chef Mrs. Reed Gardner of Carthage, Missouri, who won fourth prize with it in the vegetable category of Woodall's 1969 Open Fire Camp Cooking contest.

SCOUT RICE

4 tablespoons fat
1 cup raw rice (not instant)
1 onion, peeled and chopped
1 green pepper, chopped
1 teaspoon salt

1 teaspoon chili powder
1 can tomatoes (medium size)
1½ cups water
1 cup grated cheese (American, or your choice)

Preheat Dutch oven over hot coals. Add fat and heat. Add rice and brown, stirring constantly. Add onion and cook over coals until onion is light brown. Add green pepper, seasonings, tomatoes and water. Place lid on oven and cover with hot coals. Cook until rice is tender, about 15 to 30 minutes. Add more water if needed. Mix in cheese lightly before serving. Serves 6.

Sure—canned baked beans are good. But you're missing a treat if you don't try baking beans yourself once in a while.

DUTCH OVEN BEANS

2 pounds dry beans (Great
  Northern or Navy)
ham bone with meat
2 onions, chopped
2 cups celery, chopped

1 bay leaf
½ cup parsley, chopped
½ cup catsup
2 teaspoons salt
½ teaspoon Tabasco sauce

Soak beans overnight in water. Place all ingredients in cold Dutch oven. Add water to one inch from top. Place lid on oven and cover with hot coals. Cook for about 3 hours. Discard bay leaf before serving. Serves 8 to 10.

PIONEER BAKED BEANS

2 cups Navy beans
2 quarts water
½ cup molasses
¼ cup catsup
1½ teaspoons salt

¼ teaspoon cinnamon
1 teaspoon dry mustard
¼ pound salt pork
1 onion, peeled and sliced

Preheat Dutch oven over hot coals. Place 2 quarts of water in oven, add beans, and cook over hot coals (uncovered) for 2 hours. Drain and save water. Combine water with molasses, catsup, salt, spices and salt pork. Add drained beans and place beans and liquid in Dutch oven. Place lid on oven and cover with hot coals. Cook for about 3 more hours. Add more liquid if needed. Serves 6 to 8.

Pity the potato—it's the victim of a bad press. Most people believe that the potato is so high in caloric value that to eat one is to get fat. This isn't true, since one medium-size potato has only about 100 calories. Potatoes themselves aren't fattening—it's the butter, cheese and cream that you put on them that are. Now that we've cleared that up, here's a recipe for Scalloped Potatoes that calls for all sorts of yummy, fattening ingredients.

DUTCH OVEN SCALLOPED POTATOES

6 potatoes, pared and sliced
salt and pepper
1 cup grated cheese
4 tablespoons butter or margarine

2 eggs
2 cups milk
¼ teaspoon nutmeg

Season potatoes with salt and pepper and place in cold Dutch oven in layers, alternating with cheese. Dot each layer with butter or margarine. Beat eggs into milk, add nutmeg. Pour over potatoes and dot with remaining butter. Place lid on oven and cover with hot coals. Cook for about 1 hour, or until potatoes are tender.

Serves 4 to 6.

QUICK BREADS AND DESSERTS IN A DUTCH OVEN

Bake tender, flaky biscuits in a Dutch oven by using a prepared biscuit mix or refrigerated biscuit dough. Better yet, start from scratch and create your own.

SCRATCH BISCUITS

2 cups sifted all-purpose flour	¼ cup shortening
3 teaspoons baking powder	⅔ cup milk
1 teaspoon salt	

Preheat Dutch oven over hot coals. Sift dry ingredients together. Blend in shortening with fork. Add enough milk to form soft dough. Place dough on floured board and knead for 1 minute (or use a floured pastry cloth on your picnic table). Roll or pat dough to ½-inch thickness and cut with floured biscuit cutter. Place biscuits in lightly greased oven. Place lid on oven and cover with hot coals. Cook for about 15 minutes. Makes 12 biscuits.

If you're the parent of a Girl or Boy Scout, chances are you'll make your Dutch oven biscuits this way.

SCOUT BISCUITS

2 cups biscuit mix	⅔ cup milk

Preheat Dutch oven over hot coals. Combine biscuit mix with milk, blending well with a fork. Drop mixture by spoonfuls into lightly greased oven. Place lid on oven and cover with hot coals. Bake for about 15 minutes.

To vary this recipe, try Onion Biscuits.

ONION BISCUITS

2 cups biscuit mix
⅔ cup milk

4 tablespoons dry onion soup
   mix
⅓ cup butter or margarine

Mix biscuit mix as directed in Scout Biscuits, adding 2 table-spoons of dry onion soup mix to biscuit mix. Melt butter or margarine and add remaining 2 tablespoons dry onion soup mix. Drop biscuit mix by spoonfuls into lightly greased oven and top with butter–soup mixture. Place lid on oven, cover with hot coals and bake for about 10 minutes. Remove lid, turn each biscuit, cover and continue baking for about 10 more minutes.

Delicious desserts are the final fillip to a perfect campsite dinner. Master Campfire Chef Mrs. I. W. Adams, of Odessa, Texas, won second prize in the dessert category of Woodall's 1969 Open Fire Camp Cooking contest with this recipe for elegant Carmel Peach Crunch.

CARAMEL PEACH CRUNCH

1 cup flour
1¾ cups uncooked rolled oats
1½ cups brown sugar
1 teaspoon cinnamon

1 teaspoon salt
1 cup margarine, melted
2 large cans sliced peaches,
   drained

Line Dutch oven with aluminum foil and preheat over coals. Combine all ingredients except peaches. Blend well, and place mixture in oven on foil. Add drained peaches. Place lid on oven and cover with hot coals. Cook for about 30 to 45 minutes.

Another winner in Woodall's 1969 Camp Cooking contest was Master Camper Chef Mrs. Marcella S. Andre of Alamogordo, New Mexico, who won eighth prize in the dessert category with this recipe for Peach Cobbler.

PEACH COBBLER

¼ pound margarine
1 cup self-rising flour
1 cup sugar

1 cup sweet milk
1 large can peaches, sliced
Cinnamon (optional)

Line Dutch oven with aluminum foil and preheat over coals. Melt margarine in oven. Mix flour, sugar and milk and pour over melted fat. On top of this pour 1 large can of peaches with juice and sprinkle with cinnamon if desired. Place lid on oven and cover with hot coals. Cook for about 1 hour.

Here's another Master Campfire Chef contest winner, Mrs. Evald A. Holm of Spokane, Washington, who won thirteenth prize in the dessert category with this recipe for Rhubarb Cobbler.

RHUBARB COBBLER

1½ cups fresh, sweetened
   rhubarb
1½ cups water

½ cup sugar
1 cup biscuit mix
⅓ cup milk

Cook rhubarb in water for 5 minutes on camp stove. Place mixture in lightly greased Dutch oven preheated over coals. Combine sugar, biscuit mix and milk. Stir until dough holds together. Drop biscuit dough by spoonfuls onto hot rhubarb. Place lid on oven and cover with hot coals. Cook for about 15 to 20 minutes.

Blueberry Slump is an old-fashioned dessert that's extra good when you pick your own berries.

BLUEBERRY SLUMP

4 cups blueberries, cleaned
   and washed
1½ cups sugar
4 tablespoons cornstarch
1 teaspoon nutmeg
4 tablespoons sugar

3 tablespoons shortening
½ cup milk
1½ cups sifted flour
1½ teaspoon baking powder
¼ teaspoon salt

In large mixing bowl combine berries, sugar, cornstarch and nutmeg. Place in Dutch oven and bring mixture to boil over hot coals (without lid). Cream sugar with shortening, add milk and blend well. Mix sifted flour with baking powder and salt. Stir into shortening–sugar mixture. Drop batter by spoonfuls over hot berries. Place lid on Dutch oven and cover with hot coals. Cook for about 15 to 20 minutes.

8
Breads and Breakfast

For QUICK ENERGY and a sense of well-being throughout the morning, each new camping day should begin with a good, nourishing breakfast.

Easy-to-prepare foods, such as bacon and eggs, dry or instant cereals, pancake mixes, fresh fruits, fruit juices and milk can be toted to camp or purchased along the way, and their main contribution, after fasting through the night, is to raise your blood sugar level and thus keep your active outdoor family going until lunch time.

To add variety to your breakfast menu, here are a few campsite breakfast dishes that are high in energy value and loaded with appetite appeal.

Eggs are rich in food value and contain both proteins and vitamins. Fried in a little butter or margarine and served with bread toasted over a campfire they make a delicious breakfast treat. If you'd like to try something different, however, here are several egg dishes that will turn breakfast into something extra special.

EGGS INDIAN STYLE

4 slices bacon
1 small onion, minced
1 1-pound can whole-kernel
  corn

4 eggs
½ cup dairy sour cream
salt and pepper
dash Worcestershire sauce

Fry bacon until crisp; drain and keep warm. Leave 2 table-spoons of drippings in the pan and add onion and corn; cook, stirring often, until slightly browned. Beat eggs with sour cream and seasonings. Pour onto corn mixture and scramble gently. After cooking serve with crumbled bacon over top. Serves 4.

EGGS RANCHERO

6 slices bacon
½ cup chopped onion
⅓ cup chopped green pepper
8 eggs, beaten

1 10½-ounce can condensed
  cream of chicken soup
salt and pepper

Fry bacon until crisp; drain and crumble. In two tablespoons of bacon drippings sauté onion and green pepper until tender. Blend eggs with soup, seasonings and bacon and pour mixture into skillet with onion and green pepper. Cook over low heat until eggs are set, stirring occasionally. Serves 4.

WESTERN OMELET

¼ cup chopped ham
¼ cup chopped green pepper
¼ cup chopped onion
¼ cup butter or margarine

8 eggs
1 10½-ounce can condensed
  cream of celery soup

Combine ham, green pepper and onion with butter or margarine and cook until tender. Blend eggs with soup and add to ham mixture. Cook over low heat until eggs are set, stirring occasionally. Serves 4.

If the kitchen in your camping rig is equipped with an oven, or if you pack a portable camp oven, try these recipes for easy soufflés.

THREE-STEP SOUFFLÉ

1 10¾-ounce can condensed Cheddar cheese soup	2 tablespoons chopped chives 6 eggs, separated

Heat soup in saucepan, stirring, and add chives; remove from heat. Beat egg yolks until thick and blend into soup. In a large bowl, beat egg whites until stiff. Fold egg whites into soup mixture and pour into a 1½-quart casserole. Bake in a 300°F. oven for about 1 hour. Serves 4 to 6.

CHEESE-MUSHROOM SOUFFLÉ

4 slices bacon 1 10½-ounce can condensed cream of mushroom soup	8 ounces Cheddar cheese, cubed dash pepper 5 eggs, separated

Fry bacon until crisp; drain and crumble. Heat soup with cheese and pepper until cheese melts. Beat egg yolks until thick and blend with soup mixture. Cook slowly until thickened. Beat egg whites until stiff and fold into soup mixture. Pour into

1½-quart casserole and sprinkle with bacon crumbs. Bake into 300°F. oven for about 45 minutes. Serves 4 to 6.

What could be nicer than to climb out of a cozy sleeping bag and find your Junior Campfire Chef whipping up a little something for breakfast—warm, delicious French toast.

SKILLET FRENCH TOAST

2 eggs	3 tablespoons butter or
½ cup milk	margarine
¼ teaspoon salt	4 or 5 slices bread

Beat eggs until blended; mix in milk and salt and pour mixture into a shallow dish. Melt butter or margarine in large skillet. Dip bread into egg mixture and cook in hot fat. Turn to brown on both sides. Serve with warm syrup or confectioners' sugar.

For an even more delectable taste treat, serve French toast with Orange Syrup.

ORANGE SYRUP

1½ cups maple-blended syrup	1 tablespoon grated orange
¼ cup butter or margarine	rind (or 1 tablespoon orange juice)

Combine syrup with butter or margarine and orange rind or

juice in saucepan and bring to a boil; simmer over low heat for about 5 minutes.

BREAKFAST IN A SKILLET

8 slices Canadian bacon	2 cups cooked potatoes, cubed
3 tbsp. bacon fat	4 or 5 eggs, beaten
1 tbsp. chopped onion	1/8 tsp. pepper

Brown the bacon on both sides, remove from skillet. Leave about 3 tablespoons of fat in skillet. Add the onions, stir until limp. Add the potatoes and brown. When potatoes are nearly as brown as wanted, add the eggs, pepper and salt. Stir carefully until eggs are done and very lightly browned. Toasted, well-buttered English muffins go well with this dish. **Note:** Frankfurters cut in thin rounds or thin-sliced ham may be used in place of the Canadian bacon. Corned beef or luncheon meat could be substituted in a pinch.

Pancake mixes, especially the ones that come in packages with their own shakers, are easy to use and turn out pancakes that are fluffy, light and delicious.

For variety, roll cooked pancakes around cooked pork sausage links . . . Or blend a can of whole kernel corn into your batter . . . or blend chopped, peeled apple slices.

BUCKWHEAT GRIDDLECAKES

1/2 package (1 and 1/2 teaspoons) active dry yeast
1 1/2 cups plus 1 tbsp. lukewarm warm water
1/4 tsp. salt

2 1/2 cups buckwheat flour
1 cup milk scalded, cooled to lukewarm
1/2 tsp. baking soda

Before you go to bed, dissolve the yeast in one and one-half cups of water. Combine the flour, salt, yeast and milk in a glass, stainless steel or good plastic bowl. Beat well, cover and set in warm place.

The next morning, dissolve the soda in the tablespoon of water and add it to the batter. Test the batter by pouring a little on your hot griddle. If the batter is too thin, add a little buckwheat flour, if it's too thick, thin with warm water or milk.

Makes 2 to 3 dozen griddlecakes, depending on size. Serve with maple syrup or other syrup, honey or jam. Have butter handy, too.

POTATO PANCAKES

1 cup instant mashed potatoes
2 tablespoons grated onion
1/2 teaspoon salt
dash pepper

2 tablespoons flour
1 egg, beaten
1/4 cup salad oil

Prepare potatoes according to directions on package. Blend with onion, salt, pepper, flour and egg. Heat oil in heavy skillet. Drop two or three spoonfuls of the potato mixture into hot fat. Fry until brown on one side, turn and fry second side.

For today's campsite chef, time is an important commodity. Here are several delightful breakfast treats that take only minutes to prepare.

QUICK RAISIN TREATS

1 8-ounce package refrigerated   cream cheese
   biscuits   raisins

Flatten biscuits with fingers. Mix softened cream cheese with raisins and place a spoonful in the center of each biscuit. Fold dough up and around filling. Bake in hot 400°F. oven for about 10 mintues. Makes 10 biscuits.

QUICK COFFEE CAKE

1 9-ounce package   2 tablespoons sugar
   bake-and-serve dinner rolls   1 tablespoon chopped nuts
1 tablespoon butter or
   margarine

Place unseparated rolls on baking sheet and brush with softened butter or margarine. Sprinkle with sugar and nuts. Bake in hot 400°F. oven about 10 minutes. Slice and serve.

BUTTERSCOTCH BUNS

¼ cup butter or margarine   1 8-ounce tube refrigerated
½ cup light brown sugar   biscuits
⅓ cup chopped nuts

Soften butter or margarine and mix with sugar. Spoon butter—

sugar mixture into muffin cups, placing about 1 teaspoonful in each. Top with chopped nuts. Press a biscuit down into each cup. Bake in a hot 400°F. oven for about 10 minutes. Leave biscuits in pan about 5 minutes to cool, then turn out and serve.

PEAR CAKE

3 tablespoons butter or margarine	fresh pears, peeled, cored and halved
¼ cup brown sugar	1 package of muffin mix

Melt butter or margarine in 9-inch pan. Sprinkle with brown sugar. Arrange pears over mixture. Prepare muffin mix according to directions on package. Top pears with batter. Bake for about 30 minutes in a moderate 350°F. oven.

Cooking has always been one of my favorite hobbies, and until our waistlines started bulging, I loved to dazzle my family with all sorts of baked goods—especially loaves of tender and delicious homemade bread. Watching their eyes light up when I served those luscious loaves more than made up for the effort it took.

However, my love affair with a cake of yeast came to an end once I discovered packaged hot roll mix. No more double sifting and double rising for me.

Best of all, with hot roll mix the fragrance of homemade bread hot from the oven can easily become a part of your camp cooking adventure. Just prepare the bread or rolls following the directions on the package. Or, if you'd like to try something a little different, prepare hot roll mix this way.

CHEESE ROLLS

1 package hot roll mix
1 8-ounce package cream
  cheese
¼ cup sugar
3 tablespoons flour

1 egg yolk
1 tablespoon lemon juice
½ cup jam
chopped nuts

Prepare hot roll mix according to package directions. Turn out on lightly floured board and knead until smooth (or use pastry cloth on your picnic table). Place in greased bowl, lightly grease the top of mixture and let mixture rise in a warm place. Soften cheese; add sugar and beat until fluffy. Blend in flour, egg yolk and lemon juice.

Roll dough into a 15-inch square and cut into 25 3-inch squares. Place each square on a lightly greased baking sheet. Put 1 teaspoonful of cheese mixture in the center of each square. Bring the two diagonally opposite corners to the center of each square, overlap slightly and pinch four corners together. Cover and let rise about 30 minutes, or until doubled in bulk. Bake in a moderate 375°F. oven for about 12 minutes. Heat jam in saucepan and brush on hot rolls. Top with nuts and serve.

RAISIN WREATH

1 package hot roll mix
½ cup butter or margarine
chopped nuts

¾ cup chopped raisins
1 cup confectioners' sugar
4 teaspoons milk

Prepare hot roll mix according to directions on package. Turn out on lightly floured board and knead until smooth. Put in greased bowl, grease top of mixture and let rise in warm place until doubled in bulk. Cream softened butter or margarine and blend with nuts and raisins. Roll dough to a 24" x 10" size and spread with raisin filling. Roll up lengthwise as for jelly roll and place on lightly greased baking sheet. Shape loaf into a ring and make cuts 2 inches apart on the top. Cover and let rise for about 45 minutes. Bake in a moderate 350°F. oven for about 30 minutes. Cool and frost with a blend of confectioners' sugar and milk.

This coffeecake recipe takes a bit of preparation time, but the ingredients make it a real "family pleaser." To save time, make it at home, freeze it and then reheat it in your camp oven. Or, if your family enjoys a hike before breakfast, beg off some morning, pour a second cup of coffee and put your culinary skills to work.

PEANUT COFFEE CAKE

⅔ cup chopped salted peanuts
½ cup sugar
2 tablespoons flour
2 tablespoons cocoa
½ teaspoon cinnamon
¼ cup melted butter or
   margarine

2 cups sifted flour
¾ cup sugar
1 tablespoon baking powder
½ teaspoon soda
½ teaspoon salt
2 eggs
1 cup dairy sour cream

Combine peanuts with ½ cup sugar, 2 tablespoons flour, cocoa and cinnamon. Blend in melted butter or margarine and stir until all ingredients are moistened; set aside. In large bowl, sift flour with ¾ cup sugar, baking powder, soda and salt. In another bowl, beat eggs and blend in sour cream. Add sifted dry ingredients to egg mixture and stir until well mixed.

Spread half the batter in a greased 9-inch pan. Sprinkle with half the peanut filling. Spoon remaining batter carefully over filling. Top with remaining filling and bake in 350°F. oven for about 30 minutes. Cut into squares and serve warm.

Although sourdough is believed to be the oldest of all leavened breads, and dates as far back as 4000 B.C., it is more readily identified with America and the early West. Old-time prospectors and miners were nicknamed "sourdoughs," because they carried pots of sourdough starter so they could make bread without having to walk fifty miles for a bit of yeast.

Sourdough bread is tricky to make because it depends on a starter—a self-perpetuating yeast mixture made with flour, salt, sugar, yeast and water. Commercial starters are available, but you can also start your own from scratch.

SOURDOUGH STARTER

2 cups flour
1 teaspoon salt
3 tablespoon sugar

½ teaspoon active dry yeast
2 cups lukewarm water

Combine all ingredients and place in a large glass jar (do not use a metal container); stir until mixture forms a smooth, thin paste. Cover jar and set in a warm place to sour; stir several times a day. (Don't cap the starter jar too tightly—it could explode.) In two or three days the starter will be ready to use. Store it in your refrigerator, and at least once a week keep it active by adding 1 cup unsifted flour and 1 cup of warm water. Then let it stand at room temperature for a day.

You can increase the amount of water and flour added each

time as long as you keep the same proportions. Use your sourdough starter to make a variety of baked goods, but always reserve ½ cup or more of the starter as a base to make more.

SOURDOUGH BREAD

1 cup sourdough starter (page 103)	3 tablespoons sugar
2 cups lukewarm water	2 teaspoons salt
2½ cups sifted flour	1 package active dry yeast
1 cup milk	¼ cup warm water
3 tablespoons butter or margarine	6½ cups sifted flour
	1 teaspoon baking soda
	vegetable oil

Measure starter into large glass bowl; add 2 cups of lukewarm water and 2½ cups of sifted flour. Mix well and let stand, covered, in a warm place overnight. The next morning heat milk and stir in butter or margarine and 2 tablespoons of sugar. Blend and add salt. Cool to lukewarm. Sprinkle yeast over ¼ cup of warm water and let stand 5 minutes. Stir yeast into cooled milk mixture; add to starter mixture and beat with wooden spoon until well mixed. Beat in 2 cups of flour until batter is smooth. Mix baking soda with remaining tablespoon of sugar. Sift evenly over dough; stir gently to mix well.

Let dough rise, covered, in a warm place until double in bulk, about 40 minutes. Punch down dough; gradually beat in remaining flour until dough is stiff and cleans the sides of the bowl. Knead the dough for about 5 minutes until smooth and elastic. Divide dough in half; let rest, covered about 10 minutes. Grease bottoms of two 9″ x 5″ x 3″ loaf pans. Shape loaves and place in pans. Brush tops with vegetable oil. Let rise about 1 hour or until dough has risen to top of pans. Bake in preheated 375°F. oven about 50 minutes. Makes two loaves.

9
Soups
and Sauces

Full-bodied soup is a satisfying brew. Serve it at noon for a substantial campsite lunch, at night for a quick-cooked main dish, or in the morning as a hearty breakfast eye-opener.

Today's convenience soups make it possible for the camp chef to serve rich blends that rival the qualities of soups made at home from scratch.

To help you create a new file of time-saving campsite soup dishes, here are several recipes that feature different combinations of convenience soups—including a few robust soups made with the addition of cooked vegetables, meat, seafood or chicken.

We've also included in this chapter recipes for creamy sauces that will enhance campsite vegetable and main dish foods.

DOUBLE CHICKEN

1 10½-ounce can condensed
   cream of chicken soup

1 10½-ounce can chicken
   with rice soup
1½ soup cans of milk

Combine the soups with the milk; heat and stir. Serves 4.

CHEESE SOUP

1 10½-ounce can condensed
   Cheddar cheese soup

1 10½-ounce can condensed
   tomato soup
1½ soup cans of water

Combine soups with the water; heat and stir. Serves 4.

POTPOURRI

1 10½-ounce can condensed
   beef broth
1 10½-ounce can condensed
   green pea soup

1 10½-ounce can condensed
   tomato soup
1 soup can milk

Combine soups with the milk; heat and stir. Serve with crumbled bacon, if desired. Serves 4 to 6

SCOUT SOUP

1 10½-ounce can condensed
   Cheddar cheese soup
1 10½-ounce can condensed
   cream of celery soup
1 10½-ounce can condensed
   cream of chicken soup

1 10½-ounce can condensed
   cream of potato soup
2½ soup cans water
2 12-ounce cans Mexicorn
dash pepper

Combine soups with water. Add corn and pepper. Heat; stir. Serves 10.

CHILDREN'S DELIGHT

1 10½-ounce can condensed
   cream of celery soup
1 10½-ounce can condensed
   vegetarian vegetable soup

1½ soup cans water
buttered popcorn

Combine soups with water, Heat; stir. Pour into mugs or bowls and float popcorn on top. Serves 4.

SOUP PROVENÇAL

1 10½-ounce can condensed
   green pea soup

½ cup sour cream
1 cup water

Combine soup with sour cream; slowly stir in water. Heat, but do not boil; stir. Serves 2 to 3.

LEMON BROTH

2 10½-ounce cans condensed
   beef consommé
1½ soup cans water

2 tablespoons lemon juice
6 to 8 lemon slices

Combine consommé with water and heat to boiling. Remove from heat and stir in lemon juice. Simmer 5 minutes and serve hot with lemon slices on top. Serves 6 to 8.

SOUP ORIENTAL

2 cans chicken broth

1 egg, slightly beaten

Heat chicken broth to boiling. Remove from heat and pour in beaten egg slowly, stirring constantly. Replace over heat and cook until the egg cooks and separates into shreds. Serves 4.

ROSY SOUP

1 10½-ounce can condensed
    cream of chicken soup
1 10½-ounce can condensed
    tomato soup

2 soup cans of milk
¼ cup processed shredded
    cheese

Combine soups with milk. Add cheese and heat until cheese melts. Serves 4.

Soup becomes a main dish when it's the basis for a hearty chowder or pottage.

SARASOTA CHOWDER

1 10½-ounce can condensed
    cream of vegetable soup
2 tablespoons chopped onion
1 tablespoon butter or
    margarine

1 soup can of water
½ cup cooked diced shrimp
¼ cup chopped canned
    tomatoes

Sauté onion in butter or margarine until tender. Blend in soup and water. Add shrimp and tomatoes. Heat; stir occasionally. serves 2 to 3.

CRABMEAT SOUP

1 10½-ounce can condensed
  cream of celery soup
½ soup can milk
½ soup can water

½ cup cooked diced crabmeat
¼ cup shredded process
  cheese
sliced stuffed olives

Combine soup with milk and water. Add crabmeat and cheese. Heat until cheese melts; stir occasionally. Garnish with olives. Serves 2 to 3.

QUICK PACIFIC CHOWDER

1 10½-ounce can condensed
  cream of celery soup
1 10½-ounce can condensed
  tomato soup
1½ soup cans water
1 7-ounce can tuna, drained
  and flaked

2 tablespoons chopped onion
2 tablespoons chopped green
  pepper
1 tablespoon butter or
  margarine

Sauté onion and green pepper in butter or margarine until tender. Add remaining ingredients. Heat; stirring occasionally. Serve with crackers. Serves 4 to 5.

VEGETABLE KETTLE

1 10½-ounce can condensed
  cream of chicken soup
1 10½-ounce can condensed
  chicken vegetable soup

2 soup cans water
½ cup diced cooked bologna
1 tablespoon butter or
  margarine

Cook bologna in butter or margarine until brown. Blend

soups with water; stir in to bologna–butter mixture. Heat; stir often. Serves 4 to 6.

FRANKLY, IT'S SOUP

4 frankfurters, sliced thin
1 tablespoon butter or
    margarine
1 10½-ounce can condensed
    bean with bacon soup
1 10½-ounce can condensed
    vegetable soup
2 soup cans of water

Brown frank slices in butter or margarine. Stir in bean with bacon soup; add water and blend well. Add vegetable soup. Heat, stirring often. Serves 4 to 6.

VEGETABLE NOODLE POTAGE

1 10½-ounce can condensed
    noodle and ground beef
    soup
1 10½-ounce can condensed
    vegetable beef soup
1½ soup cans water
¼ cup chopped onion
½ cup chopped cabbage
2 tablespoons butter or
    margarine
shredded process cheese

Sauté onion and cabbage in butter or margarine; cook until brown and tender. Add soups and water. Heat, stirring often. Garnish each serving with cheese. Serves 4 to 5.

CHICKEN CHOWDER

1 10½-ounce can condensed
    cream of celery soup
1 10½-ounce can condensed
    chicken vegetable soup

1½ soup cans water
1 cup cooked, diced chicken
¼ cup cooked corn
¼ cup chopped canned
   tomatoes

4 slices bacon
¼ cup chopped onion
¼ cup sliced mushrooms
dash pepper

Cook bacon until crisp; drain and crumble. Pour off all but 2 tablespoons of drippings. Sauté onion and mushrooms in bacon drippings; cook until onion is tender. Add remaining ingredients. Heat; stir often. Garnish with crumbled bacon. Serves 4 to 5.

Dress up a campsite meal with easy-to-fix sauces that turn "Plain Jane" foods into gourmet treats.

MEAT SAUCES

TOMATO SAUCE

1 10½-ounce can condensed
   tomato soup

1 tablespoon Worcestershire
   sauce
1 tablespoon lemon juice

Heat soup; add Worcestershire and lemon juice. Serve over frankfurters or corned beef hash. Makes 1¼ cups of sauce.

MUSTARD SAUCE

3 tablespoons butter or
   margarine

3 tablespoons flour
½ teaspoon salt

beef broth | sugar

¼ cup prepared
horseradish–mustard

Melt butter or margarine in small saucepan. Stir in flour and salt. Cook, stirring often, until bubbly. Add beef broth and continue cooking and stirring until sauce thickens—about 1 minute. Stir in horseradish–mustard and brown sugar. Serve over ham, pork or tongue. Makes 1⅔ cups of sauce.

POULTRY SAUCE

2 tablespoons onion, chopped
1 tablespoon butter or
   margarine

1 10½-ounce can condensed
   cream of chicken soup
⅓ cup milk
2 teaspoons lemon juice

Sauté onion in butter or margarine. Combine soup with milk and heat. Add browned onion and lemon juice. Heat and stir often. Makes about 1½ cups of sauce.

SEAFOOD DRESSING

1 cup dairy sour cream
1 tablespoon minced onion
⅔ teaspoon curry powder

½ teaspoon salt
few drops hot pepper sauce

Combine above ingredients; blend well. Serve with tuna, salmon, shrimp, crab or lobster salad. Makes about 1 cup of dressing.

VEGETABLE SAUCES

QUICK HOLLANDAISE

1 10½-ounce can condensed
  cream of celery soup
½ cup milk

2 tablespoons butter or
  margarine
2 tablespoons lemon juice
2 egg yolks, slightly beaten

Combine all ingredients and heat over low heat until thickened, stirring constantly. Do not boil. Makes 1⅔ cups sauce.

THE FASTEST SAUCE IN THE WEST

1 10½-ounce can condensed
  cream of asparagus soup

⅓ cup milk

Blend soup with milk; heat and serve over vegetables. Makes about 1 cup of sauce.

CHEESIE SAUCE

1 10½-ounce can condensed
  Cheddar cheese soup
¼ cup milk

½ cup chopped canned
  tomatoes, drained

Combine soup with milk and tomatoes. Heat; stirring often. Makes about 1 cup of sauce.

CREAMY SAUCE

1 10½-ounce can condensed
   cream of celery soup
¼ cup of milk

1 3-ounce package softened
   cream cheese

Blend softened cheese with soup; add milk. Heat; stir often. Serve over cooked peas and carrots. Makes about 1½ cups of sauce.

DESSERT SAUCES

APRICOT SAUCE

1 1-pound 14-ounce can
   apricot halves
¾ cup sugar

¼ cup orange juice
dash salt
½ teaspoon almond extract

Drain apricots, saving ½ cup of syrup. Dice apricots and stir in reserved syrup. Add sugar, orange juice and salt. Cook mixture slowly for about 10 minutes, stirring occasionally. Stir in almond extract: Chill before serving.

GOLDEN DESSERT SAUCE

¼ cup sugar
½ cup fruit juice
2 tablespoons lemon juice
1 teaspoon butter or margarine

2 egg yolks, lightly beaten
1 cup prepared whipped
   topping

Combine sugar with lemon juice and butter or margarine along with your own favorite fruit juice. Heat until sugar dissolves, stirring occasionally. Lightly beat egg yolks and stir a small amount of the hot sugar mixture into the yolks; blend well. Return yolks to remaining hot mixture and continue cooking until thickened, about one minute. Remove from heat and beat well. Place in camp cooler or refrigerator and chill. Before using, fold in prepared whipped topping. A perfect sauce for gingerbread, fresh or cooked fruit, cake or pound cake. Sauce may be stored in camp cooler or refrigerator for several days.

10
Salads,
Dressings
and Relishes

IF YOU LIKE to play with colors and textures when you're preparing your family's campsite meals, try your creative skills with salads.

It's fun to arrange plates of tempting salad greens topped with a colorful display of fruits or vegetables, served with a rich yellow dressing or a creamy white sauce.

To facilitate salad making in camp, we carry cleaned salad fixings for raw salads the first few days and use canned cooked vegetables for salads when fresh foods aren't available.

For best results, raw salads should be tossed with dressing just before eating, but the ingredients can be prepared ahead of time and stored in a tightly sealed plastic bag in your camp cooler or galley refrigerator. Vegetable salads can also be made ahead of time and refrigerated for later serving.

Meat, fish or poultry salads are easily prepared in a camp kitchen and make a satisfying and filling campsite meal.

Fruit salads can be served before, or with a campsite meal—and they're also marvelous as a campsite dessert.

So whether you're a calorie-conscious camper or a hearty eater, satisfy an outdoor appetite with a nutritious, appetizing salad. We offer the following recipes as suggestions for salads—and we're certain that the chef in your family will want to add his or her own variations.

Raw Salads

For a well-balanced camping menu, and to add sparkle to the most conventional campsite meal, complement your main dish with a nutritious, energy-packed raw salad rich in vitamins and minerals.

VITAMIN C SALAD

lettuce leaves, washed
3 tomatoes, peeled and sliced
1 cucumber, pared and sliced
1 green pepper, sliced
1 medium onion, sliced
2 tablespoons chopped parsley

DRESSING
½ cup salad oil
¼ cup lemon juice
1 clove garlic, peeled, split
1½ teaspoon salt
10 drops Tabasco

Make dressing first by combining all ingredients. Pour mixture into large glass jar, cover and shake; chill.

In salad bowl, arrange lettuce leaves and top with sliced tomatoes, cucumber, green pepper and onion. Sprinkle with parsley and chill. Before serving, remove garlic from dressing; shake again. Pour dressing over vegetables and toss. Serves 6.

WESTERN SALAD

½ medium-size head lettuce, washed and shredded
1 small red apple, halved, cored and sliced

½ small Bermuda onion, peeled and sliced
½ cup sliced celery
½ cup bottled French dressing

Combine lettuce, apple, onion and celery in large bowl.

Drizzle French dressing over top and toss lightly to mix. Serves 6.

SCOUT SALAD

1 small head of cabbage, shredded
3 stalks celery, diced

3 carrots, diced
mayonnaise

Combine shredded cabbage with diced celery and carrots. Add mayonnaise to moisten and toss lightly to mix. Serves 4.

CARROT AND RAISIN SALAD

4 cups grated, pared carrots
1 cup raisins
½ cup mayonnaise

1 teaspoon lemon juice
1 tablespoon milk
lettuce leaves, washed

Combine carrots and raisins. Mix mayonnaise, lemon juice and milk; add to carrots and raisins. Serve on lettuce leaves. Serves 6.

Delight the small fry with carrot broomsticks.

CARROT BROOMSTICKS

3-inch carrot sticks
5-inch carrot sticks

sliced green olives

Gather several 3-inch carrot sticks and slip a green olive ring over them to hold them together. Poke a 5-inch stick through for the broom handle.

CHILI COTTAGE CHEESE SALAD

1 pint cottage cheese
1 cup ripe olives, chopped
1 cup cubed cucumber
1 tablespoon lemon juice
1 teaspoon instant minced
  onion

½ teaspoon salt
dash pepper
dash chili powder
salad greens
2 large tomatoes, sliced
whole ripe olives for garnish

Combine all ingredients except salad greens, tomato slices and whole ripe olives. Arrange greens on large plate; top with cottage cheese mixture and garnish with tomato slices and whole ripe olives. Serves 4 to 6.

PICKLE-EGG SALAD

8 eggs, hard-cooked and
  chilled
¼ cup chopped sweet gherkins

½ cup salad dressing
1 teaspoon prepared mustard
salad greens

Cut eggs into large chunks. Mix with chopped pickles, salad dressing and mustard. Serve on a plate of salad greens. Serves 4.

When buying cabbage at a farm stand or a supermarket, look for firmly packed heads with thick, pale-green leaves. Wash head thoroughly and then shred it to make this perennial favorite: cole slaw.

COLE SLAW SUPREME

4 cups finely shredded cabbage
¼ cup sugar
¼ teaspoon salt
⅛ teaspoon dry mustard

⅛ teaspoon pepper
½ cup evaporated milk
¼ cup cider vinegar

Combine sugar, salt, dry mustard and pepper with evaporated milk in small bowl. Let stand for about 5 minutes, stirring occasionally to dissolve sugar. Gradually blend in cider vinegar; chill. Before serving pour chilled mixture over shredded cabbage and toss lightly. Serves 6 to 8.

OLD-FASHIONED COLE SLAW

2½ cups shredded cabbage
2 tablespoons chopped parsley
1 tablespoon chopped onion
1 tablespoon chopped
  pimiento

DRESSING
2 slices bacon
½ cup mayonnaise
2 tablespoons vinegar
½ teaspoon salt

Fry bacon until crisp, drain and crumble. Combine mayonnaise with vinegar, salt and crumbled bacon. In large bowl, place shredded cabbage, parsley, onion and pimiento. Stir mayonnaise mixture into cabbage mixture and toss lightly. Serves 4.

Vegetable Salads

Cut down on camp cooking chores! Salads made with canned, cooked vegetables serve as a salad and a vegetable dish—and most of them can be prepared ahead of time and stored in your camp cooler or galley refrigerator.

CHUCK WAGON SALAD

1 1-pound can barbecue beans	dash pepper
2 stalks celery, diced	salad greens
¼ cup chopped green pepper	cucumber slices
¼ teaspoon salt	mayonnaise thinned wtih milk

In large bowl, combine beans, celery, green pepper, salt and pepper; chill. Arrange salad greens on large plate. Place a circle of cucumber slices on greens; top with chilled beans. Garnish with mayonnaise thinned to the desired consistency with milk. Serves 4.

THREE-BEAN SALAD

1 1-pound can cut green beans, drained	⅓ cup cider vinegar
1 1-pound can wax beans, drained	4 teaspoons cornstarch
	1 teaspoon salt
1 1-pound can kidney beans, drained	2 cups sliced celery
	½ cup thinly sliced green onions
1 cup apple jelly	

Combine 3 varieties of beans in large bowl. Blend jelly with vinegar, cornstarch and salt in heavy pan. Cook until thick, stirring frequently. Cool. Mix jelly mixture with beans; chill. Toss celery and onions with mixture before serving. Serves 12.

CAMPFIRE SALAD

1 1-pound can cut green
  beans, drained
1 15-ounce can sliced small
  tomatoes, drained

3 cups shredded lettuce
½ cup bottled Thousand
  Island dressing

Mix beans and tomatoes; chill. Place lettuce in large bowl; cover with chilled beans and tomato mixture. Spoon dressing over tomatoes and toss before serving. Serves 6.

KIDNEY BEAN SALAD

3 cups cooked red kidney
  beans
1 cup diced celery
4 hard-cooked eggs, diced
4 green onions sliced thin

¼ cup piccalilli relish
1 cup diced cold potato
salt and pepper to taste
mayonnaise

Combine all ingredients and season to taste with salt and pepper. Chill before serving. Serves 8.

KIDNEY BEAN SALAD II

1 1-pound can red kidney
  beans, drained
4 hard-cooked eggs,
  cut in chunks
1 onion, minced
1 green pepper, chopped

1 carrot, shredded
1 4½-ounce can deviled ham
¼ cup sweet pickle relish
mayonnaise
salad greens

Combine all ingredients except mayonnaise and salad greens.

Chill. Before serving add mayonnaise to moisten, serve on plate of salad greens. Serves 4.

KRISPY KRAUT

1 1-pound can sauerkraut
1 2-ounce can sliced
   pimientos, drained
½ cup chopped green onions
¾ cup sliced celery
1 cup shredded carrots
1 green pepper, sliced

¼ cup vinegar
½ cup sugar
¾ teaspoon salt
dash pepper
lettuce, tomato wedges
   (optional)

Drain sauerkraut. In a large bowl, combine kraut with pimiento, onions, celery, carrots and green pepper. In another bowl, mix vinegar, sugar, salt and pepper; stir until sugar is dissolved. Pour vinegar mixture over sauerkraut mixture. Mix to combine, cover and refrigerate. Keeps well in a camp cooler for about 8 hours. If desired serve salad in lettuce-lined bowl and garnish with tomato wedges. Serves 8.

NUTTY SALAD

1 1-pound can peas, drained
½ cup salted peanuts
½ cup chopped dill pickle

½ cup bottled clear French
   dressing
lettuce leaves

Drain peas and toss with salted peanuts, chopped dill pickle and French dressing. Chill. Serve on lettuce leaves. Serves 6.

We freely admit that in camp, potato salad can be a major production—especially if you're trying to boil potatoes, cook eggs and fry bacon all at the same time on a two-burner camp stove. Potato salad is an appetizing dish, however, and because we enjoy it as an accompaniment to cold ham, meat loaf or grilled hamburgers, we precook the potatoes and eggs at home and combine them with the rest of the ingredients after arriving at camp. Here are several recipes for flavorful potato salad that can be prepared in camp with precooked potatoes.

COUNTRY POTATOES

1 pound bacon
3 pounds precooked potatoes,
   peeled and diced
1 medium green pepper,
   chopped

1 bunch celery, chopped
mayonnaise
piccalilli

Fry bacon until crisp; drain and crumble. In large bowl, combine bacon with precooked diced potatoes. Add green pepper and celery. Combine mayonnaise with piccalilli to desired taste, pour over potato–bacon mixture. Chill. Serves 6 to 8.

HOT EGG-POTATO SALAD

6 hard-cooked eggs, chopped
4 cups precooked, diced
   potatoes
2 tablespoons butter or
   margarine
2 tablespoons flour
1½ teaspoons salt

pepper to taste
1 cup milk
1 medium onion, minced
1 canned pimiento, chopped
1 cup diced celery
⅔ cup mayonnaise

Melt butter or margarine in large skillet; blend in flour and seasonings. Gradually add milk and cook until thickened, stirring occasionally. Add potatoes and heat. Before serving, add remaining ingredients, saving some of the chopped eggs for garnish. Mix lightly and top with reserved eggs. Serve hot. Serves 4.

For an easy potato salad, try this recipe:

QUICK POTATO SALAD

2 pounds precooked, diced
  potatoes
1 onion, sliced thin

3 tablespoons minced parsley
1 cup mayonnaise

Mix diced potatoes with onion slices. Add two tablespoons of parsley to the mayonnaise and blend with potato–onion mixture. Garnish with remaining 1 tablespoon of parsley. Serves 4 to 6.

Variations

Substitute French dressing for mayonnaise . . . combine Thousand Island dressing with mayonnaise . . . combine sour cream with mayonnaise.

Cottage cheese adds extra nourishment to potato salad. To each three cups of potatoes used add 2 cups of creamed cottage cheese.

MAIN COURSE SALADS

When you're camping during the summer, at the peak of the salad-growing season, center lazy campsite meals around a nutritious main-course salad served with crackers or cocktail rye and topped off with tall refreshing glasses of iced tea or lemonade.

DO-IT-YOURSELF SALAD

1 small head lettuce, washed and shredded
1 hard-cooked egg, quartered
1 cup cooked ham cut into strips

1 cup cooked diced chicken
1 cup cubed Cheddar cheese
Swiss cheese cut into strips
mayonnaise or salad dressing

Place shredded lettuce on large plate. Arrange egg, ham, chicken and cheeses side by side. Serve with mayonnaise or your own favorite salad dressing. Serves 4 to 6.

TUNA SURPRISE

1 7-ounce package elbow macaroni
1 medium head lettuce, washed and shredded
1 medium carrot, shredded
8 small radishes, sliced

1 8-ounce can green beans, drained
2 hard-cooked eggs, sliced
1 13-ounce can waterpack tuna, drained
Orange Dressing

Cook macaroni in boiling, salted water about 8 minutes until tender. Drain; rinse with cold water and drain again. Combine lettuce, carrot, radish slices, green beans and egg slices with drained tuna fish; add cooked macaroni and blend well. Serve with Low-Calorie Orange Dressing (see below). Serves 10.

LOW-CALORIE ORANGE DRESSING

1 cup orange juice

½ teaspoon oregano

2 teaspoons minced onion
1 teaspoon seasoned salt
1 teaspoon cider vinegar
⅛ teaspoon pepper

Combine all ingredients and place in glass jar; cover and shake until blended. Add dressing to salad.

QUICK TUNA SALAD

2 7-ounce cans tuna
2 hard-cooked eggs, diced
1 cup chopped celery
⅓ cup mayonnaise
few drops Tabasco
lettuce leaves, washed
chopped ripe olives for garnish
  (optional)

Drain and flake tuna. Combine with eggs, celery, mayonnaise and Tabasco. Serve on lettuce leaves and garnish with chopped ripe olives, if desired. Serves 4.

TANGY CHICKEN SALAD

1 cup diced cooked chicken
¾ cup sliced celery
6 tablespoons sour cream
salt and pepper to taste
lettuce leaves, washed

Combine all ingredients except lettuce; serve on lettuce leaves. Serves 4.

EGG AND FRANK SALAD

½ pound frankfurters, sliced
2 tablespoons margarine
4 eggs, hard-cooked and cut
  into chunks
5 cups sliced cooked potatoes
1 onion, minced

DRESSING
1½ teaspoons flour
1 tablespoon sugar
1 teaspoon salt

½ cup vinegar
½ cup water
3 tablespoons margarine

In a saucepan, blend flour, sugar, salt, vinegar and water with three tablespoons of margarine. Cook, stirring, until thickened. Cook franks in 2 tablespoons of margarine until browned. In a large bowl, combine egg chunks and diced potatoes with onion. Add hot sliced franks and hot vinegar–water mixture. Blend well and serve hot. Serves 4 to 6.

A main course salad is a beautiful way to satisfy hearty outdoor appetites and keep calorie intake to a minimum. A one-cup serving of the following salad, which combines apples with ham and cabbage, contains only 130 calories.

HAM-APPLE SALAD

¾ cup cooked ham, cut in
  strips
1½ cups unpeeled, diced
  apples

1 cup slivered red cabbage
1 cup slivered green cabbage
2 stalks celery, diced
salt and pepper

Combine all ingredients and toss lightly. Serve with low-calorie buttermilk dressing (see below). Serves 4 to 6.

BUTTERMILK DRESSING

3 tablespoons lemon juice
1¼ teaspoons seasoned salt
1 cup buttermilk

⅛ teaspoon prepared mustard
2 teaspoons sugar

Combine all ingredients except sugar; blend well. Add sugar Makes 1 cup of dressing; 1 tablespoon contains only 8 calories. Serve with Ham-Apple Salad.

FRUIT SALADS

Apples from Washington and Oregon, cherries from Wisconsin and Michigan, grapes from California and New York, oranges and grapefruit from California and Florida and peaches from Georgia are just a few of the delectable fruits that campers can sample as they travel through each section of our beautiful country.

For a delicious campsite snack, serve fresh fruits whole or cut in wedges and arranged on a plate. Or use them as the basic ingredient for a mouth-watering fruit salad.

PEACH-NUT SALAD

½ pint small curd cottage cheese
2 tablespoons chopped maraschino cherries
7 tablespoons chopped walnuts

lettuce head, washed
4 peaches, pared, pitted and halved
sour cream or mayonnaise

Combine cottage cheese, cherries and walnuts. With a sharp knife, cut 4 slices crosswise from head of lettuce and arrange sections on serving plates. Top each section with two peach halves; fill peach centers with cottage cheese mixture. Top with sour cream or mayonnaise. Serves 4

FRUIT SALAD BOWL

1 melon	4 slices of pineapple
2 pears	2 bananas
4 peaches	

Peel and cut melon into wedges. Peel and core pears and peaches; cut into chunks. Cut pineapple into bite- sized pieces; peel and slice bananas. Combine all ingredients in large bowl. Serve with Really Good Dressing (see below) or any fruit dressing. Serves 6.

REALLY GOOD DRESSING

2 tablespoons sugar	1 tablespoon lemon juice
1 teaspoon dry mustard	1 teaspoon grated onion
1 teaspoon paprika	¼ teaspoon Worcestershire
¼ teaspoon salt	sauce
5 tablespoons vinegar	1 cup salad oil

Combine all ingredients except for salad oil and blend well. Add salad oil and blend again.

Each summer during cherry-picking time, we plan a weekend campout in northern Wisconsin where some of our country's sweetest cherries are harvested. After feasting on several pints of fresh-picked fruit, we tote the rest home to be prepared for our freezer. We're especially fond of this camping dessert, made by combining fresh cherries with ripe, chilled cantaloupe.

CHERRY-MELON SALAD

2 ripe cantaloupes, chilled   lettuce leaves, washed
2 cups fresh red cherries, pitted   mayonnaise

Cut both cantalope into halves crosswise and remove seeds. Cut one into balls with a melon scoop; the other slice thin. Arrange lettuce leaves in large bowl. Combine cantaloupe balls and cherries and place in center of the bowl. Arrange cantaloupe slices around the cherry mixture. Serve with mayonnaise. Serves 6.

Banana Salad is delightful when served with a fish or a chicken dish.

BANANA SALAD

3 bananas, peeled   ½ cup seedless grapes
lemon juice   ¼ cup finely chopped salted
¾ cup cooked, chilled rice   peanuts
¼ cup sliced celery

Peel bananas and cut into ½-inch slices; sprinkle with lemon juice. Combine banana slices with cooked rice, celery, grapes and peanuts. Serve with Banana Salad Dressing (see below) Serves 6

BANANA SALAD DRESSING

½ cup mayonnaise   ½ teaspoon dry mustard
1 tablespoon milk   ½ teaspoon curry powder
1 tablespoon lemon juice

Combine all ingredients, blend well. Add to Banana Salad and toss lightly.

To make a quick fruit salad with little preparation time, substitute canned, cooked fruit for fresh.

NANCY'S FRUIT SALAD

1 large can fruit salad,
   drained
marshmallows cut into pieces

sour cream
lettuce leaves, washed

Combine drained fruit salad with marshallow pieces. Moisten with sour cream; serve on lettuce leaves. Serves 4 to 6.

SUN SPOTS

1 cup mayonnaise
3-ounce package cream cheese
lettuce leaves, washed

6 large slices canned pineapple
6 canned peach halves
6 maraschino cherries

Combine mayonnaise with cream cheese; blend well. Arrange lettuce leaves on six individual plates and top with one pineapple slice. Place a peach half hollow-side up over each pineapple slice; fill peach centers with mayonnaise-cream cheese mixture. Top with cherry. Serves 6.

DRESSINGS AND RELISHES

Perk up the flavor of salads and add a personal touch by dressing them with your own campmade salad dressing. In camp, without the convenience of a blender, mix your dressing in a glass jar. Pour all the ingredients into the jar, cover tightly and shake until well blended. If you don't use all the dressing at one meal, store the jar in your camp cooler or refrigerator and use it again tomorrow.

QUICK RUSSIAN DRESSING

1 10½-ounce can condensed cream of celery soup
¼ cup mayonnaise
¼ cup chili sauce
1 teaspoon lemon juice
1 tablespoon minced onion

Mix all ingredients together and pour into large jar. Cover and shake until blended. Makes about 1¾ cups dressing.

TOMATO-BLUE CHEESE DRESSING

1 10½-ounce can condensed tomato soup
¼ cup vinegar
¼ cup crumbled blue cheese
½ cup salad oil
1 tablespoon minced onion
2 tablespoons sugar
2 teaspoons dry mustard
1 teaspoon salt
¼ teaspoon pepper

Combine all ingredients in a 1-quart jar and shake well. Chill before serving. Makes about 2¼ cups of dressing.

Variations

Add leftover pineapple syrup to mayonnaise and use for dressing fruit salad.

Add a little prepared mustard to mayonnaise and use for dressing egg salad.

Relish adds an interesting flavor to meats, poultry and fish. Here are several relishes that can be made quickly in a camp kitchen.

QUICK CORN RELISH

1 12-ounce can whole kernel corn, drained
¼ cup corn liquid
1 cup sweet pickle relish

sliced green onions to taste
2 diced pimientos
1 tablespoon sugar

Combine ingredients in saucepan; cover and simmer for about 15 minutes. Serve hot or cold.

UNCOOKED TOMATO RELISH

3 pounds tomatoes, peeled and chopped
¾ cup chopped onion
¾ cup chopped celery
¾ cup chopped green pepper

2 teaspoons salt
3 tablespoons sugar
¼ teaspoon nutmeg
¼ teaspoon cinnamon
¼ teaspoon ground cloves
1 cup cider vinegar

Combine all ingredients. Pack into jars, cover and place in camp cooler. Relish will keep, refrigerated, for about three weeks. Makes about 2 quarts of relish.

PINEAPPLE-APPLE RELISH

½ cup diced celery
boiling water
1 13½-ounce can pineapple
    tidbits, drained

2½ cups canned applesauce
½ teaspoon ground ginger
1 teaspoon grated orange rind

Cover celery with boiling water and let stand for about 5 minutes. Drain. Combine remaining ingredients with celery and simmer for about 15 minutes. Cool; chill. Makes 4 cups of relish.

11
Vegetable Dishes

Fresh or cooked, vegetables are among the most nutritious foods the camp chef can serve her family—and the least expensive!

Vegetables supply sugar for energy, they're a good source of calcium and they also contain an impressive amount of vitamins needed to keep active campers healthy.

With a minimum amount of effort, vegetables can be turned into delectable side dishes that make splendid partners for the grilled, roasted or fried main dish.

Balance your family's diet with generous daily portions of vegetables, and for variety, choose from the following collection of easy-to-prepare dishes.

Fresh or canned string beans are a flavorful campsite treat when they're combined with french fried onions and served with barbecued chicken or hamburgers.

GREEN BEAN CASSEROLE

2 1-pound cans French-style green beans

2 10½-ounce cans condensed cream of mushroom soup

¼ teaspoon pepper   1 can french fried onions

In a 2-quart casserole, combine soup, beans, pepper and ½ can of french fried onions. Bake in galley oven at 350° F. for about 15 minutes, or until contents are bubbling. Top with remaining french fried onions and bake for 5 minutes longer. Serves 6.

Try combining beans with Sloppy Joe mix for a different flavor combination.

DEVILED GREEN BEANS

2 1-pound cans French-style   1 cup water
  green beans   1 6-ounce can tomato paste
1 package Sloppy Joe   1 cup shredded Cheddar
  seasoning mix   cheese

Combine seasoning mix and water in small saucepan. Bring to boil, and stir until sauce is thickened. Add tomato paste. Drain beans and add to seasoning mixture. Pour into 1½-quart casserole, sprinkle with cheese and bake in galley oven at 350° F. for about 20 minutes, or until cheese is melted. Serves 6.

Here's a lima bean recipe that's a perfect accessory for any grilled or barbecued meat dish.

LIMA BEANS AND BACON

2 1-pound cans lima beans,   3 slices bacon
  drained   1 chopped onion

1 garlic clove, crushed
1 teaspoon prepared mustard
½ teaspoon Worcestershire
   sauce
¼ teaspoon chili powder
1 small can tomato sauce
1 tablespoon vinegar

Fry bacon until crisp, drain and crumble. In 2 tablespoons of bacon drippings, sauté onion and garlic until tender. Blend in mustard, Worcestershire, chili powder, tomato sauce and vinegar. Add drained lima beans, cover and simmer for about 10 minutes. Before serving top with crumbled bacon. Serves 6.

Carrots are so nutritious and good for you that if you just eat one each day you'll more than fulfill your daily quota of Vitamin A. Fresh or canned, carrots are the basic ingredient of several campsite vegetable dishes that we find especially delicious.

GLAZED CARROTS

16 small carrots
1½ teaspoons melted butter
   or margarine
4 teaspoons sugar

Scrape carrots and cook whole, covered, in boiling salted water until tender, or about 10 minutes. Drain off cooking liquid. Add melted butter or margarine and sugar, carefully tipping pan until carrots are glazed. Serves 6 to 8.

Variation

To cook carrots, add melted butter or margarine and sprinkle with 4 tablespoons of brown sugar and a dash of nutmeg. Cover and cook over low heat until carrots are glazed.

ORANGE CARROTS

2 cups sliced carrots
½ cup orange juice

2 tablespoons butter or
  margarine
¼ teaspoon salt

Place carrots in saucepan; add orange juice, butter or margarine and salt. Cover and cook over quick heat until liquid evaporates; brown slightly in additional butter, if desired. Serves 4

Tender, juicy ears of sweet corn, rolled in melted butter and seasoned with salt, can make vegetarians out of beef-eating campers. Sweet corn can be prepared in a variety of ways. It can be roasted in foil (see Aluminum Foil cooking page 27), it can be grilled over a campfire (see Grilling and Barbecuing page 170)—or, to bring out all the delicate flavor, you can slip husked corn into a kettle and cook it in boiling water

KETTLE CORN

In a large kettle, bring to a rapid boil enough water to cover corn. Remove husks and silk from corn and place in boiling water. Cover and cook until tender, about 10 minutes. To boost the flavor, add a tablespoon of sugar per gallon of water.

For a special taste treat, serve hot boiled corn with seasoned corn butter.

SEASONED CORN BUTTER

½ cup butter   1 teaspoon ground oregano

Soften butter and blend in ground oregano. Serve with sweet corn.

When fresh sweet corn isn't available, canned corn is a delicious accompaniment for campsite suppers, either heated and served with butter and salt or combined with other canned foods in savory casserole dishes.

TOMATO CORN

1 12-ounce can whole kernel   1 tablespoon butter or
  corn   margarine
1 14½-ounce can sliced baby   salt and pepper
  tomatoes

Drain corn and place in lightly greased casserole. Drain tomatoes and arrange over corn. Dot with butter or margarine and season to taste with salt and pepper. Bake in galley oven at 350° F. for about 30 minutes. Serves 6.

CORN, BY CRACKY

1 1-pound can whole kernel   1 10½-ounce can condensed
  corn   cream mushroom soup

1 tablespoon minced onion
dash pepper
1 cup crumbled soda crackers

2 tablespoons butter or
margarine

Drain corn. Combine soup with onion and pepper. In 1-quart casserole, arrange alternate layers of corn, soup mixture and crumbled crackers. Dot with butter or margarine and bake in galley oven at 400° F. for about 25 minutes. Serves 6.

CREAMED CORN AND BEANS

1 1-pound can whole kernel
corn, drained
1 1-pound can cut green
beans, drained

1 10½-ounce can condensed
Cheddar cheese soup
milk

Combine drained corn and beans; stir in soup. Heat mixture and thin to desired consistency with milk. Season to taste. Serves 6 to 8.

CORNY CHOWDER

1 2-ounce package á la
king sauce mix
3 cups milk

1 12-ounce can whole kernel
corn
2 tablespoons instant minced
onion

In large pan, empty contents of sauce mix package; stir in milk. Add corn and onion and heat to boiling over medium heat, stirring constantly. Serves 4 to 5.

For campers who feel that no meal is complete without

a potato, here are several recipes for potato dishes that are easily made in camp.

CAMPFIRE POTATOES AND TOMATOES

4 medium potatoes
2 medium tomatoes
1 medium onion
½ green pepper
2 tablespoons salad oil

4 tablespoons butter or
  margarine
½ teaspoon salt
dash pepper
½ teaspoon sugar

Preboil potatoes, cool, pare and cut into ½-inch dice. Peel tomatoes, cut in half and dice. Peel and slice onion thin; seed the green pepper and slice thin.

In heavy skillet, heat salad oil and two tablespoons of butter or margarine. Sauté the diced potatoes slowly, cooking until golden; season with salt and pepper. In another small pan, sauté the onion, green pepper and tomato in the remaining two tablespoons of butter or margarine until soft, but not brown. Sprinkle with sugar and keep warm. Turn cooked potatoes into serving dish and cover with warm tomato mixture. Serves 6 to 8.

QUICK PARSLEYED POTATOES

2 1-pound cans whole white
  potatoes
4 tablespoons butter or
  margarine

1 teaspoon salt
1 teaspoon pepper
¼ cup chopped parsley

Drain and slice potatoes. Heat skillet and melt butter or margarine; sauté potatoes in hot fat; season with salt and pepper. Cook for about 15 minutes, or until potatoes are browned; add parsley and serve. Serves 6.

ONION SPUDS

4 cups cold, cooked, diced
  potatoes
⅔ cup butter or margarine

1 teaspoon salt
dash pepper
2 cups onions, thinly sliced

In large skillet, melt ⅓ cup butter or margarine; add potatoes and season with salt and pepper. Cook for about 20 minutes, or until browned. In another pan, melt remaining ⅓ cup butter and add onions; cook until soft and browned. Add onions to potatoes, mixing well, and heat through. Serves 4.

SKILLET SCALLOPED POTATOES

4 potatoes, peeled and thinly
  sliced
1 small onion, chopped
1½ cups milk
½ teaspoon salt
dash pepper

1 tablespoon catsup
½ teaspoon Worcestershire
  sauce
¾ cup diced process American
  cheese
1 tablespoon margarine

Arrange sliced potatoes in heavy skillet. Blend onion, milk, salt, pepper, catsup and Worcestershire and pour over potatoes. Add cheese and margarine and bring mixture to boil; cover and simmer for about 1 hour, or until potatoes are tender. Turn occasionally. Serves 4.

Canned sweet potatoes taste like homemade when you make them in camp with this recipe.

SWEETS WITH MARSHMALLOWS

1 large can sweet potatoes
3 tablespoons butter or
  margarine

salt
½ cup milk
marshmallows

Mash and season sweet potatoes with butter or margarine and salt. Blend in milk. Place in lightly greased casserole and cover with marshmallows. Bake in galley oven at 350° F. until marshmallows are puffed brown.

Today's convenience foods make campsite meal preparation a breeze. Here are several recipes that take advantage of processed potatoes.

INSTANT POTATO CASSEROLE

8 to 10 servings instant
  mashed potatoes
1 cup dairy sour cream

1 cup shredded, process
  American cheese

Heat galley oven to 400° F. and prepare potatoes according to directions on package, omitting milk. Blend in sour cream and pour mixture into a 1-quart casserole. Sprinkle with cheese and bake for about 15 minutes. Serves 8.

POTATO SOUFFLÉ

8 servings instant mashed
  potatoes
6 eggs, separated

¾ cup shredded Parmesan
  cheese
½ teaspoon salt

Prepare instant mashed potatoes according to directions on package. While hot, beat in egg yolks, then blend in cheese. Let mixture cool. Whip egg whites until stiff, add salt and fold beaten whites into cooled potato mixture. Spoon mixture into a lightly greased 2-quart casserole and bake in your galley oven at 375° F. for about 45 minutes. Serves 8 to 10.

ROADSIDE SPUDS

4 to 5 servings instant mashed potatoes
2 eggs, separated

½ cup packaged bread crumbs
2 tablespoons butter or margarine

Prepare potatoes according to directions on package, omitting milk. Beat in egg yolks and blend well. Place potato mixture in camp cooler or refrigerator and let stand until lunch. Place egg whites in covered jar in cooler also. At noon, bring out potato mixture and shape into 8 patties. Bring out egg whites and dip patties into whites, then into dish of packaged crumbs. Heat butter or margarine in heavy skillet and cook patties in hot fat until golden brown on the bottom. Turn and brown second side.
Serves 4.

Plump, ripe tomatoes, peeled and sliced, are a delicious companion to grilled meats and poultry. Serve them with your own favorite dressing, or try this easy-to-fix sauce.

GARLIC TOMATOES

4 medium tomatoes
⅓ cup salad oil
2 tablespoons vinegar

1 clove garlic, mashed
salt and pepper

Peel and slice tomatoes and arrange on shallow platter. Combine remaining ingredients. Sprinkle tomatoes with mixture and chill for about 1 hour before serving. Serves 4.

Zucchini, a tender member of the squash family, is featured in this delightful campsite vegetable dish.

SKILLET ZUCCHINI

2 medium-sized zucchini
3 tablespoons salad oil
1 clove garlic, mashed
1 teaspoon oregano

¾ teaspon salt
¼ teaspoon sugar
dash pepper

Slice zucchini into ¼-inch thick pieces. In large skillet, heat oil and sauté garlic for about 3 minutes. Add zucchini slices and cook, uncovered, for about 10 minutes, stirring occasionally. Add a mixture of oregano, salt, sugar and pepper, and continue cooking for about 5 minutes longer, or until zucchini is tender. Serves 4 to 6.

Coax the youngest campers into eating vegetables by serving them with a cream sauce. Here's a recipe for a speedy sauce that can be used with canned string beans, carrots, peas, potatoes or spinach.

VEGETABLES IN CREAM SAUCE

3 cups cooked vegetables   milk
1 10½-ounce can condensed
   cream of celery, chicken or
   mushroom soup

Stir cooked vegetables into 1 can of soup; heat and thin to desired consistency with milk. Serves 6.

12
Cooking
Inside Your Rig . . .
Casseroles and
Skillet Meals

IF YOU'RE the new owner of a modern recreational vehicle, you'll soon discover there's an infinite variety of attractive foods that can be prepared using the efficient built-in kitchen appliances found inside your camping rig.

Since there are many times when it's easier and more convenient to cook a complete meal indoors, we've included in this chapter a selection of main course dishes, including casseroles and skillet meals, that can be prepared using your rig's built-in range and oven.

Some are quick-as-a-flash recipes, while others take a little longer to prepare—but few take more than an hour preparation and cooking time.

MEAT CASSEROLES

AN EASY BEEF PIE

3 12-ounce cans roast beef
   with gravy

1 12-ounce can whole kernel
   corn

½ cup sliced cooked carrots
1 can refrigerated butterflake
   dinner rolls

2 tablespoons melted butter or
   margarine
¼ cup grated Parmesan cheese

Combine roast beef, corn, and carrots in casserole, mixing well. Separate rolls and arrange around the edge. Brush with melted butter or margarine; sprinkle with grated cheese. Bake in preheated 350° F. oven for 15 minutes. Serves 5.

CORNED BEEF–CABBAGE CASSEROLE

1 cup diced cooked corned
   beef
4 cups coarsely shredded
   cabbage

1 10½-ounce can condensed
   cream of celery soup
½ cup chopped onion
1 teaspoon dry mustard

Combine all ingredients in 1½-quart casserole. Cover with sheet of aluminum foil. Bake in preheated 350° F. oven 45 minutes. Serves 4.

INSTANT CASSEROLE

1 can beef stew
instant mashed potatoes

grated cheese

Empty beef stew into casserole; prepare instant mashed potatoes for 2; add prepared potatoes top of stew. Sprinkle grated cheese over all. Bake in preheated 350° F. oven for 30 minutes.

CHILI BEEF CASSEROLE

2 tablespoons butter or
   margarine

1 onion, chopped
1 pound ground beef

1 teaspoon salt
¼ teaspoon chili powder

½ cup seedless raisins
1 1-pound can creamstyle corn

Melt butter or margarine in large skillet; add onion and sauté for 5 minutes. Add beef; cook, stirring occasionally, until meat loses red color. Stir in salt, chili powder and raisins. Cook about 2 minutes, stir in corn. Turn mixture into 1½-quart casserole; bake in preheated 350° F. oven for 25 minutes. Serves 4.

BEEF-MAC CASSEROLE

2 tablespoons vegetable oil
1 onion, chopped
1½ pounds ground beef
2 teaspoons salt
½ teaspoon pepper
½ cup grated Parmesan
  cheese
2 tablespoons butter or
  margarine
2 tablespoons flour
½ teaspoon salt

¼ teaspoon pepper
2 teaspoons Worcestershire
  sauce
2 cups milk
¼ cup grated Parmesan
  cheese
4 tomatoes, sliced
1 8-ounce package elbow
  macaroni, cooked and
  drained

Heat vegetable oil in large skillet. Add onion and beef; cook 5 minutes, stirring occasionally. Stir in 2 teaspoons salt, ½ teaspoon pepper and cook 5 minutes. Stir in ½ cup Parmesan cheese.

In saucepan, melt butter or margarine, remove from heat and blend in flour, ½ teaspoon salt, ¼ teaspoon pepper and Worcestershire. Stir in milk gradually. Cook over medium heat, stirring, until thick. Boil 1 minute, remove from heat and stir in ¼ cup Parmesan cheese.

In greased 3-quart casserole, layer half the meat mixture,

cover with tomatoes and noodles. Pour half the sauce over mixture. Repeat layers; pour on remaining sauce. Bake in preheated 375° F. oven for 30 minutes. Serves 6.

HAM-WHAT-AM CASSEROLE

1 tablespoon butter or margarine
¼ cup chopped onion
1 tablespoon chopped green pepper
1 10-ounce can condensed Cheddar cheese soup
½ cup milk
2 cups cooked macaroni
1 cup diced cooked ham
2 tablespoons buttered bread crumbs

In skillet, melt butter or margarine and sauté onion and green pepper until tender. Blend in soup; gradually stir in milk. In buttered 1-quart casserole, combine sauce, cooked macaroni and ham. Sprinkle crumbs over top. Bake in preheated 375° F. oven for 30 minutes. Serves 4.

PORK CHOP POTATO SCALLOP

4 pork chops
1 10½-ounce can condensed cream of mushroom soup
½ cup sour cream
¼ cup water
4 cups thin-sliced potatoes
salt and pepper

Brown chops in skillet. Blend in soup, sour cream, water. Turn mixture into 2-quart casserole, alternating with layers of potatoes seasoned with salt and pepper. Top layer should be chops and sauce. Cover with sheet of aluminum foil; bake in preheated 375° F. oven for 1 hour. Serves 4.

SOUR CREAM BEEF AND NOODLE CASSEROLE

4 tablespoons butter or margarine
1 pound ground beef
2 cups sliced onion
1 clove garlic, minced
1 teaspoon salt
¼ teaspoon pepper
1 tablespoon flour
1 3-ounce can sliced mushrooms

1 tablespoon Worcestershire sauce
1 beef bouillon cube
1 cup dairy sour cream
1 6½-ounce package noodles, cooked and drained
½ cup grated Parmesan cheese

Melt 2 tablespoons butter or margarine in skillet; add beef, onion and garlic; cook until onion is soft and meat crumbly. Add salt, pepper and flour; blend well. Add mushrooms with liquid; blend, and then add Worcestershire and bouillon cube, mixing well. Stir in sour cream. Combine cooked noodles with ¼ cup cheese, 2 tablespoons melted butter, stir.

In 1½-quart casserole, arrange alternate layers of noodle and meat mixtures. Cover and bake in preheated 350° F. oven 25 minutes. Uncover and sprinkle with remaining ¼ cup cheese. Return to oven for 5 minutes uncovered. Serves 6.

Poultry Casseroles

CHICKEN BAKE

2 tablespoons shortening
1 cup thin-sliced celery
¼ cup chopped onion
3 10½-ounce cans condensed
   cream of chicken soup

1½ cups milk
3 cups diced cooked chicken
3 cups cooked noodles
¼ cup buttered bread crumbs

Heat shortening in skillet; sauté celery and onion until tender. Blend in soup and milk. Add chicken and noodles. Pour into greased 1½-quart casserole; top with buttered bread crumbs. Bake in preheated 375° F. oven 45 minutes. Serves 8.

EASY CHICKEN PIE

1 can condensed cream of
   mushroom soup
½ soup can water
2 tablespoons minced onion
dash pepper
1 cup cooked chicken, cubed
¾ cup cooked carrot strips

¾ cup diced cooked potato
1 cup biscuit mix
¼ teaspoon dehydrated onion
   flakes
⅓ cup milk
2 tablespoons bread crumbs

Combine soup, water, onion and pepper in 1½-quart casserole; add chicken, carrots and potato. Bake in preheated 450° F. oven for 15 minutes. Combine biscuit mix, onion flakes and milk. Roll dough to fit top of casserole. Place on hot chicken mixture; prick with fork; sprinkle with 2 tablespoons bread crumbs. Return to oven and bake 15 minutes longer. Serves 4.

CRUNCHY TUNA CASSEROLE

1 10½-ounce can condensed
   cream of mushroom soup
½ cup milk
1 7-ounce can tuna, drained
   and flaked

2 hard-cooked eggs, sliced
1 cup cooked peas
½ cup crumbled chow mein
   noodles

Combine soup and milk in 1-quart casserole; stir in tuna. Add eggs and peas. Bake in preheated 350° F. oven for 25 minutes. Top with noodles, return to oven and bake 5 minutes longer. Serves 4.

CRABBY CASSEROLE

1½ cups cooked crab meat
1 cup cooked rice
1½ cups stewed tomatoes
½ cup mushroom pieces
1 6-ounce can tomato paste

small can drained chopped
   ripe olives
salt and pepper
1 tablespoon dried minced
   onion
buttered bread crumbs

Combine all ingredients except crumbs and place in buttered casserole; top with buttered bread crumbs. Bake in preheated 350° F. oven for 30 minutes.

SPECIALTY CASSEROLES

BUBBLY NOODLES

¼ cup chopped onion
1 tablespoon butter or
  margarine
1 10½-ounce can condensed
  Cheddar cheese soup

½ cup milk
2 cups cooked macaroni
buttered crumbs

Sauté onion in butter or margarine until tender. In large buttered casserole, blend soup, milk and cooked onion. Add cooked macaroni. Sprinkle with buttered crumbs. Bake in preheated 375° F. oven for 30 minutes. Serves 4.

OLD-FASHIONED MACARONI

1 8-ounce package macaroni
¼ cup butter or margarine
¼ cup flour
1 teaspoon salt

dash pepper
2 cups milk
2 cups grated Cheddar cheese
  (8 ounces)

Cook macaroni as directed on package; drain and set aside. Melt butter or margarine in saucepan; remove from heat and stir in flour, salt and pepper; beat until smooth. Gradually stir in milk; bring to boiling, stirring constantly. Reduce heat and simmer 1 minute; remove from heat. Stir in 1½ cups cheese and cooked macaroni. Pour into buttered 1½-quart casserole. Sprinkle remaining cheese over top. Bake, uncovered, in preheated 375° F. oven for 20 minutes. Serves 6.

ZESTY SAUSAGE CASSEROLE

1 pound pork sausage (bulk)
1 7¼-ounce packaged
  macaroni and cheese dinner
2 8-ounce cans tomato sauce

1½ cups water
2 tablespoons instant minced
  onion

Brown pork sausage, drain off fat. Cook macaroni as directed on package. In 1½-quart casserole, combine cooked macaroni, contents of cheese packet from packaged dinner, tomato sauce, water and onion. Add browned sausage. Cover with sheet of aluminum foil; bake in preheated 350° F. oven for 20 minutes. Serves 4.

POTATOES AND FRANKS

2 tablespoons butter or
  margarine
½ cup minced onion
3 tablespoons flour
1½ cups water
½ teaspoon salt

dash pepper
2 teaspoons dry mustard
½ pound frankfurters, sliced
4 cups thin-sliced, pared
  potatoes

Heat butter or margarine; sauté onion until tender. Stir in flour and cook 1 minute. Add water, salt and pepper. Bring to boil, stirring constantly. Remove from heat; blend in mustard. Butter a 1-quart casserole; place alternate layers of potatoes and franks in casserole, ending with layer of potatoes. Cover with sauce. Cover casserole with sheet of aluminum foil. Bake in preheated 375° F. oven for 40 minutes. Remove cover and bake 15 minutes longer. Serves 4.

CANADIAN BAKED BEANS

2 1-pound 14-ounce cans pork
  and beans
2 8-ounce cans tomato sauce
¼ cup brown sugar

2 tablespoons prepared
  mustard
2 tablespoons instant minced
  onion
8 slices Canadian bacon

Combine all ingredients except bacon in casserole. Arrange bacon slices on top. Bake uncovered in preheated 350° F. oven for 1 hour and 15 minutes. Serves 6 to 8.

Meal-in-a-Skillet Dishes

Earn a high "appreciation" rating from your family by varying their campsite menu with a hearty one-dish meal cooked in a skillet.

CAMPER'S TREASURE

2 8-ounce cans tomato sauce
1 1-pound can baby lima
  beans, undrained
1 1-pound can potatoes,
  drained and sliced

1 cup water
1 beef bouillon cube
1 12-ounce can roast beef
1 3½-ounce can french fried
  onion rings

Combine tomato sauce, lima beans with liquid, potatoes, water and bouillon cube in large skillet; heat and simmer 5 minutes. Cut beef into large pieces; add to vegetables and simmer. Before serving, stir in half the onion rings. Garnish each serving with remaining onion rings. Serves 6.

SKILLET MEAT PIE

1 tablespoon butter or
  margarine
1 8-ounce can whole onions,
  drained
1 10½-ounce can condensed
  vegetable soup

½ cup water
1 12-ounce can corned beef
1 cup prepared biscuit mix
⅓ cup milk

Melt butter or margarine in skillet; brown onions. Add soup, water and meat; heat. Combine biscuit mix with milk; drop by spoonfuls on hot meat. Cook uncovered 10 minutes; covered 10 minutes. Serves 4.

KENTUCKY BURGOO

2½ pounds ground beef
1 pound onions, peeled and
  chopped
3 tablespoons bacon fat
2 10½-ounce cans condensed
  tomato soup
1 10½-ounce can cream of
  celery soup

1 soup can water
½ teaspoon salt
dash pepper
1 teaspoon sugar
1 pound elbow macaroni,
  cooked and drained

Cook beef and onions in heavy skillet in bacon fat until lightly browned. Add soups and water. Add salt, pepper and sugar. Stir well, cover and simmer for 20 minutes. Stir in drained macaroni, cover and simmer 10 more minutes. Serve hot. Serves 8 to 10.

ROCKY MOUNTAIN BURGOO

2 tablespoons shortening
2½ pounds ground beef
1 teaspoon salt
2 10½-ounce cans condensed
   chili beef soup

2 10½-ounce cans condensed
   tomato soup
1 soup can water
1 pound elbow macaroni,
   cooked

Melt shortening in heavy skillet. Add beef and salt and cook until browned. Blend in soups and water. Heat, simmer for 10 minutes. Add drained macaroni; blend well. Simmer 10 more minutes. Serves 8 to 10.

QUICK SKILLET DISH

1 pound ground beef
1 onion
2 1-pound, 3½-ounce cans
   spaghetti with tomato and
   cheese

1 can Mexicana corn with
   peppers

Brown beef in skillet; drain off grease. Add remaining ingredients and simmer for about 15 minutes. Serves 4 to 5.

GOLDEN BEEF SPECIAL

1 pound ground beef
1 package chili seasoning mix
1 cup water

1½ cups shredded sharp
   natural Cheddar cheese
2 cups corn chips

Brown beef in skillet; drain off most of the grease, Stir in chili seasoning and water. Bring to boil; cover and simmer for

10 minutes. Stir in one cup of cheese; heat until just melted. Top with remaining cheese and corn chips. Serves 4 to 5.

SKILLET STEAK SUPPER

1 pound ground beef
¼ cup bread crumbs
¼ cup chopped onion
1 beaten egg
½ teaspoon salt
dash pepper

½ cup diced green pepper
1 10½-ounce can condensed vegetable soup
1 8-ounce can tomatoes, chopped

Combine beef with bread crumbs, onion, egg, salt and pepper; shape into 4 patties. Brown in skillet; push to one side. Sauté green pepper in skillet; cook until tender. Add soup and tomatoes. Return meat, cover and cook 20 minutes. Serves 4.

EASY STROGANOFF

2 tablespoons butter or margarine
1 pound round steak, cut into thin strips
½ cup chopped onion

1 10½-ounce can condensed cream of mushroom soup
¼ cup water
½ cup sour cream
½ teaspoon paprika

Melt butter or margarine in skillet. Brown strips of round steak in hot fat. Add onion and brown. Stir in soup, water, sour cream and paprika. Cover and cook over low heat about 45 minutes, or until meat is tender. Stir frequently. Serves 4.

SWEET-SOUR SKILLET

1 12-ounce can luncheon meat
1 8-ounce can tomato sauce
with onions
½ cup raisins
¼ cup water
3 tablespoons brown sugar
1 tablespoon crushed
gingersnap cookies

Cut luncheon meat into 6 slices; brown in skillet. In saucepan, combine tomato sauce, raisins, water, brown sugar and crushed gingersnaps. Heat and simmer 5 minutes. Pour sauce over browned lunch meat, simmer 5 minutes longer. Serves 4 to 5.

CAMPER'S CHOP SUEY

2 tablespoons salad oil
1 pound round steak, cut in
thin strips
1 10½-ounce can condensed
golden mushroom soup
½ cup water
1 tablespoon soy sauce
1½ cups sliced celery
1 cup green pepper, cut into
1-inch squares
½ cup green onion, cut in
1-inch pieces
cooked rice

Heat oil in skillet, add beef and brown. Add remaining ingredients except rice. Cover and cook over low heat for about 20 minutes, or until meat is tender. Stir occasionally. Serve over cooked rice. Serves 4.

SKILLET LIVER

4 slices bacon
1 pound thin-sliced beef liver
2 tablespoons flour
salt and pepper

1 10 1/2-ounce can condensed   1/2 cup sour cream
   onion soup

Cook bacon in skillet; remove and drain. Pour off all but 2 tablespoons of drippings. Dust liver with flour, season with salt and pepper. Brown in bacon drippings; add soup. Cover and cook over low heat 20 minutes, or until tender. Gradually stir in sour cream. Heat thoroughly. Serve with bacon. Serves 4.

SKILLET FISH

1/2 cup flour or bread crumbs   4 to 6 small fish
1/4 tsp. salt   Fat for frying
1/8 tsp. pepper

Put flour or crumbs in a paper bag, add the salt and pepper. Drop in the fish and shake well. In the meantime have the fat heating in a skillet. When it is hot, lay in the fish and cook for 10 minutes, turning once. An old-fashioned cast iron frying pan creates crispness.

SKILLET CHICKEN DELIGHT

1/4 cup butter or margarine   1 10 1/2-ounce can condensed
2 pounds chicken parts   chicken gumbo soup
1/4 cup flour   1/2 soup can water
                               2 tablespoons catsup

Heat butter or margarine in skillet. Flour chicken pieces; brown in hot fat. Stir in soup, water and catsup. Cover and simmer 45 minutes. Stir often. Serves 4 to 5.

SEAFOOD SKILLET

1 10½-ounce can condensed
  tomato soup
¾ cup water
⅓ cup quick-cooking rice
¼ cup instant minced onion
⅓ cup chopped green pepper

¼ teaspoon salt
1 7-ounce can tuna
4 slices processed American
  cheese, cut into thin strips
⅓ cup chopped ripe olives

Combine soup and water in skillet; heat to boiling. Stir in rice, onion, green pepper and salt. Simmer for 10 minutes. Stir in tuna. Top with cheese slices and chopped olives. Cover skillet and heat until cheese melts. Serves 5.

QUICK CAMPER'S RICE

1½-cups packaged precooked
  rice
1 16-ounce can stewed
  tomatoes
1 16-ounce can red kidney
  beans

1 cup water
1 teaspoon salt
1 teaspoon chili powder
2 4-ounce cans Vienna sausage

Combine all ingredients except sausage in skillet. Bring to boil. Add sausage and simmer uncovered about 4 minutes, or until rice is tender, stirring occasionally. Serves 6.

CAMPER'S RICE SPECIAL

1½ cups packaged precooked
  rice

1 10½-ounce can condensed
  French-style onion soup

½ cup water
1 16-ounce can whole green
  beans

1 12-ounce can corned beef,
  sliced

Combine rice, soup, water and beans in skillet. Bring to a boil. Add sliced corned beef and simmer uncovered 5 minutes, or until rice is tender. Stir occasionally. Season as desired. Serves 6.

OPEN-FIRE CHILI PEPPERS

2 8-ounce cans tomato sauce
1 12-ounce can whole kernel
  corn
1 teaspoon salt
3 medium green peppers,
  halved and seeded

1 1-pound can chili con carne
  with beans
½ cup shredded Cheddar
  cheese

Combine tomato sauce, corn and ½ teaspoon salt in large skillet; boil, then reduce heat to simmer. Arrange peppers, cut-side up, in skillet. Sprinkle peppers with remaining salt. Fill peppers with chili cover with tomato-corn sauce. Simmer, covered, 25 minutes or until tender. Sprinkle with cheese. Serves 6.

SKILLET FRIED PERCH

4 tablespoons butter or
  margarine
9 well-cleaned perch
¼ cup milk

½ cup flour (or cornmeal)
1 tablespoon lemon juice
1 teaspoon minced parsley
seasonings

Melt 2 tablespoons butter or margarine in skillet. Dip perch first in milk, then in flour—or cornmeal if you prefer. Lay perch in skillet and fry until browned, about 6 minutes on each side. Larger fish take longer. Remove fish to hot platter. Melt remaining 2 tablespoons butter or margarine in skillet. Add lemon juice and parsley and your choice of seasoning—salt, pepper, paprika or garlic powder. Heat but don't brown. Pour hot sauce over fish. Serves 4.

Hot Sandwiches

Sturdy hot sandwiches make timesaving meals for busy campers. Prepare the sandwich filling ahead of time, chill, and then heat and serve before or after sightseeing excursions.

PEANUT SLOPPY JOES

1 10½-ounce can condensed
   tomato soup
2 tablespoons lemon juice
2 tablespoons brown sugar
1 teaspoon prepared mustard
1 teaspoon Worcestershire
   sauce
2 tablespoons margarine

½ cup chopped onions
1 pound ground beef
¼ teaspoon salt
dash pepper
½ cup dry roasted peanuts,
   chopped
hamburger buns

Combine soup, lemon juice, brown sugar, mustard and Worcestershire sauce; blend well. Heat margarine; sauté onions. Add ground beef, salt and pepper; brown. Stir in soup mixture and simmer for 15 minutes. Before serving, blend in dry roasted peanuts. Serve in buns. Serves 4 to 6.

CHILI BEEF FRANKS

¼ pound ground beef
1 10½-ounce can condensed
  chili beef soup
⅓ cup water

2 teaspoons prepared mustard
1 pound frankfurters, cooked
frankfurter buns

In skillet, brown beef, stir to separate. Add soup, water and mustard; heat, stirring frequently. Place frankfurters, cooked, in buns. Spoon soup mixture over franks. Serves 8 to 10.

CHICKEN BURGERS

2 cups diced cooked chicken
1 10½-ounce can cream of
  chicken soup
1 4-ounce can sliced
  mushrooms
¼ cup chopped green pepper
¼ cup chopped onion

3 tablepoonss chopped
  pimiento
½ teaspoon MSG
½ teaspoon poultry seasoning
6 hamburger buns, split in
  halves

Combine all ingredients except buns in large mixing bowl. Spread equal amounts of mixture (about ¼ cup) on each bun half. Broil in camping rig oven about 6 inches from heat for about 7 to 10 minutes—until brown and bubbly. Makes 12 open-face burgers.

RABBIT ON TOAST

6 crisp-cooked bacon slices
1 10½-ounce can condensed
  Cheddar cheese soup

1 10½-ounce can condensed
  tomato soup
¼ cup milk

6 tomato slices   6 slices toast
6 onion slices

Cook bacon, drain off fat and set aside. In saucepan, blend cheese soup with tomato soup and milk; mix well. Heat, stir often. Arrange tomato and onion slices on toast. Cover with soup sauce. Top with bacon. Serves 6.

Here are a couple of quickie hot sandwiches the whole family will enjoy.

BROILED BACON AND TOMATO SANDWICH

8 slices cooked bacon   ⅓ cup milk
4 slices toast, buttered   1 teaspoon minced onion
8 slices tomato   ½ teaspoon Worcestershire
1 10½-ounce can condensed   sauce
   cream of mushroom soup

Fry bacon, set aside. Arrange buttered toast slices on cookie sheet. Top each with 2 slices each of tomato and bacon. Stir soup until smooth; add milk, onion and Worcestershire. Pour soup mixture over open-face sandwiches. Broil until hot and bubbly. Serves 4.

MARSHMALLOW FRUIT SANDWICH

white bread, sliced and   canned pineapple rings
   buttered   maraschino cherries, halved
American cheese slices   granulated sugar
marshmallows

Place slice of American cheese on buttered white bread. Top with marshmallow. Place pineapple ring around marshmallow. Add cherry halves to top and sprinkle with granulated sugar. Bake in a hot oven for 15 minutes, or until marshmallow has melted and toasted.

JIFFY PIZZA

6 English muffins, split and
   toasted
12 slices mozzarella cheese
12 slices bacon, cooked and
   crumbled

¼ cup finely chopped onion
1 8-ounce can tomato sauce
   with mushrooms

Split and toast muffins; butter lightly. On each muffin half place slice of cheese, crumbled bacon, chopped onion and tomato sauce. Bake in preheated 400° F. oven for 5 to 10 minutes until browned. Serves 4 to 6.

CAMPER'S PIZZA

2 8-ounce cans refrigerated
   buttermilk biscuits
1 10½-ounce can pizza sauce
1 tablespoon grated Parmesan
   cheese

¼ teaspoon garlic powder or
   oregano
½ pound shredded mozzarella
   cheese
1 4-ounce can sliced
   mushrooms, drained

Separate biscuits and flatten each into an oval about 4 inches long. On greased cookie sheet, arrange flattened biscuits side by side, touching each other in 4 long rows. In saucepan, heat pizza sauce with Parmesan cheese and garlic powder. Spread pizza sauce over biscuits. Sprinkle with mozzarella and mushroom slices. Bake 12 minutes in preheated 450° F. oven. Serve hot. Serves 6 to 8.

13
Grilling and Barbecuing

THERE'S A limitless variety of campsite foods that take on a delicious, zesty flavor when they're grilled or barbecued over hardwood or charcoal coals.

Campfire grilling, the oldest and most traditional method of campsite cookery, requires a large fire and a little patience on the part of the campsite chef. If you're in a hurry and grill your food in the flames, it will turn out crunchy black on the outside and raw on the inside. Let the flames die down to glowing embers before you grill, and your food will cook to a golden brown, well-done all the way through. (See Chapter 4, Fire Building.)

Planning to grill with charcoal? Here are a few suggestions that will help make your barbecue a rousing success.

CHARCOAL GRILLING

Charcoal grills for traveling come in tabletop or freestanding models, fold compactly, pack in a small amount of space and retail for as little as $1.50 or as much as $35.00. Most grills feature a metal or porcelainized fire bowl, chrome-plated grids, and are designed for use with either lump charcoal or charcoal briquettes.

A bed of charcoal briquettes—the most popular form of charcoal for outdoor grilling—comes to a full cooking heat about 20 minutes after lighting. For faster heating, charcoal may be started without fluid by using a metal charcoal lighter. A charcoal lighter is a tapered aluminum cylinder with vent holes in the base, a swinging grate and a detachable handle. To operate, place crumpled paper under the grate, pour charcoal in the lighter and then light the paper. Coals will be hot for cooking in about 10 minutes.

Before using a charcoal grill, place a sheet of aluminum foil or a layer of fine gravel in the bottom of the grill. Then either arrange the briquettes in a pyramid shape and light them using a commercial starting fluid, or place briquettes in fire starter and place starter on the grill. Once the briquettes have burned down to a grayish white, spread them out and you're ready for grilling.

To help add to your file of grilled and barbecued camping dishes, we offer the following easy-to-prepare recipes along with a Methods and Times chart which lists average cooking times for the most popular cuts of meat, poultry and fish suited to outdoor grilling.

Timing for Grilled Meats, Poultry and Fish

CUT	COOKING TIME
Beef	
Filet mignon or tenderloin 1-1½" thick	Grill a total of 5 to 15 minutes for rare to well done

CUT	COOKING TIME
Porterhouse 1-1½" thick	Grill a total of 6 to 15 minutes for rare to well done
T-bone 1-1½" thick	Grill a total of 6 to 15 minutes for rare to well done
Rib 1-1½" thick	Grill a total of 6 to 15 minutes for rare to well done
Club 1-1½" thick	Grill a total of 6 to 15 minutes for rare to well done
Delmonico 1-1½" thick	Grill a total of 5 to 15 minutes for rare to well done
Strip or shell 1-1½" thick	Grill a total of 5 to 15 minutes for rare to well done
Sirloin 1-1½" thick	Grill a total of 10 to 25 minutes for rare to well done
Flank 1" thick	Tenderize or marinate and grill a total of 5 to 10 minutes for rare to well done
Chuck, bone in 2" thick	Tenderize or marinate and grill a total of 10 to 25 minutes for rare to well done
Chuck, boned; round rump 2" thick	Tenderize or marinate and grill a total of 10 to 25 minutes for rare to well done
Beef cubes 1" x 1" chunks	Tenderize or marinate and skewer-grill a total of 25 to 30 minutes
Round 1-1½" thick	Tenderize or marinate and grill a total of 15 to 25 minutes for rare to well done
Short ribs	Marinate or tenderize; grill, basting with sauce, a total of 25 minutes
Ground beef	Grill a total of 5 to 15 minutes for rare to well done

CUT	COOKING TIME
PORK	
Rib, loin or shoulder chops	Marinate, grill a total of 40 minutes
Spareribs	Pre-boil; grill a total of 30 to 40 minutes
Loin	Marinate; split, roast, grill a total of 40 minutes
Precooked ham steak 1″ thick	Grill a total of 15 minutes
Ham cubes	Skewer-grill a total of 15 minutes
LAMB	
Rib chops 1-2″ thick	Grill a total of 25 minutes
Cubes	Marinate; skewer-grill a total of 20 minutes
POULTRY	
Broiling or frying chickens split or quartered	Grill, basting, if desired, a total of 45 minutes
Young turkeys split or quartered	Grill, basting, if desired, a total of 45 minutes per pound
FISH	
Whole, cleaned	Grill a total of 10 to 20 minutes
Fish steaks	Grill a total of 15 minutes

Grilled Meat, Poultry and Fish

Ask any camper over ten years old what his favorite campsite meat dish is and chances are a whopping majority of us would answer, "Steak"—juicy, tender steak grilled outdoors over coals!

Although some steaks are definitely in the luxury class, there are other cuts of meat that require only a few hours of marinating or a bit of meat tenderizer to make them suitable for outdoor grilling.

If you're splurging on the tenderest steak, merely slash through the outside fat covering at one-inch intervals to keep it from curling, and then place it on a grill about 4 inches above the coals. To determine cooking time, see timing chart (page 172).

However, if you'd like to grill some of the less tender cuts, here are a few recipes, including sauces, that will help you turn them into real barbecue treats.

Basting food with a sauce or a marinade is a cooking trick that makes the most conventional campsite dish seem new and exciting. Here are several tangy sauces that can be used with meats or poultry.

BASIC BARBECUE SAUCE

1 onion, chopped
2 tablespoons butter or
    margarine
2 tablespoons vinegar
2 tablespoons brown sugar
4 tablespoons lemon juice
1 cup catsup

3 tablespoons Worcestershire
    sauce
½ teaspoon prepared mustard
½ cup water
½ cup chopped celery
salt

In large skillet, sauté onion in melted butter or margarine. Add remaining ingredients, cover and simmer for about 30 minutes. Makes 2 cups of sauce.

MILD BARBECUE SAUCE

1 8-ounce can tomato sauce
1 tablespoon cider vinegar
½ teaspoon Worcestershire
  sauce
1 teaspoon salt
2 tablespoons vegetable oil
2 tablespoons minced onion

Blend all ingredients in saucepan; simmer for about 10 minutes stirring occasionally. Makes 1 cup of sauce.

QUICK BARBECUE SAUCE

½ cup chili sauce
1 tablespoon vinegar
1 tablespoon Worcestershire
  sauce
¾ cup water

Blend all ingredients in saucepan; simmer for about 5 minutes, stirring occasionally. Makes about 1½ cups of sauce.

SIMPLE BARBECUE SAUCE

3 tablespoons butter or
  margarine
½ teaspoon A-1 Sauce
⅛ teaspoon Worcestershire
  sauce

In saucepan, melt butter or margarine, add remaining ingredients and blend. Cook for about 5 minutes. Makes about ¼ cup sauce.

TEXAS BARBECUE SAUCE

½ cup vegetable oil
1 cup chopped onions
1 clove garlic, minced
1 20-ounce can tomatoes

1 cup water
1½ teaspoons salt
2 tablespoons chili powder
¼ cup cider vinegar

Heat 2 tablespoons of the oil in a large skillet. Sauté onions until brown. Add garlic, tomatoes, water, salt, chili powder and remaining oil. Bring to a boil and cook over low heat for about 20 minutes. Add vinegar and cook 10 minutes longer. Makes about 2¼ cups of sauce.

SOUTHERN BARBECUE SAUCE

1 14-ounce bottle tomato
  catsup
¼ pound butter or margarine
3 tablespoons lemon juice

1 clove garlic, minced
1 tablespoon Worcestershire
  sauce

Combine all ingredients in saucepan and bring to boil. Reduce heat and cook for about 10 minutes. Makes about 2¼ cups of sauce.

Inexpensive flank steak has a zippy new taste when it's marinated in a tangy barbecue sauce.

BARBECUED FLANK STEAK

1 flank steak, 1½–2 pounds
½ cup chopped onion

1 clove garlic, minced
2 tablespoons salad oil

1 can condensed beef broth
½ cup catsup
1 tablespoon brown sugar
1 tablespoon Worcestershire
  sauce

2 teaspoons prepared mustard
½ teaspoon oregano
toasted buns

Sauté onion and garlic in oil until tender. Stir in remaining ingredients except steak. Cook over low heat, stirring frequently, for about 15 minutes. Score flank steak and cover with sauce. Marinate for about 1 hour. Place steak on grill about 4 inches above hot coals and cook for about 5 minutes, basting frequently. Turn and continue basting until done, about 5 minutes more. Slice meat in thin, diagonal slices and serve on toasted buns with remaining sauce. Serves 6 to 8.

Flank steak, though less tender than porterhouse, is delicious when tenderized and prepared in this main dish.

FLANK STEAK OLÉ

2½ lbs. flank steak
Instant meat tenderizer
2 slices bacon, partially cooked
  and cubed
1 tablespoon prepared
  horseradish

1 tablespoon prepared mustard
2¾ cups water
1 envelope dry onion soup mix
2½ cups precooked rice
1½ tablespoon butter or
  margarine

Tenderize meat according to directions on package of tenderizer. Cut a gash lengthwise in steak to make a pocket. Combine bacon with horseradish and mustard. Spread mixture in pocket and secure with toothpicks. Place steak on grill about 4 inches above hot coals and broil for about 10 minutes, turning once.

Combine water and soup mix in large skillet. Bring to boil and cook over moderate heat for 5 minutes. Stir in rice and butter or margarine and bring to vigorous boil. Cook over moderate heat about 5 minutes longer. Remove steak from grill and serve with sauce. Slice steak diagonally across the grain in thin slices. Serves 5.

Chuck steak usually requires moist-heat cooking. But if you tenderize it first, it can be grilled and becomes a mouth-watering dish that rivals its more regal relative, the sirloin.

CHILI STEAK

1 arm or blade chuck steak, cut 1½ inches thick (about 3 to 3½ pounds)
1 to 2 tablespoons chili powder
1 clove garlic, sliced
½ cup sliced pimiento-stuffed olives
⅓ cup vegetable oil
¼ cup lemon juice
instant meat tenderizer

Place steak in shallow pan; sprinkle with chili powder, garlic, and olives. Combine oil with lemon juice and pour over steak. Cover and let stand 2 to 3 hours, turning steak once. Remove steak and tenderize following directions on package. Place steak on grill about 4 inches over hot coals and cook for about 30 minutes, turning once and basting frequently. Serves 4.

To add variety to your campsite menu, here's another chuck steak recipe that requires little preparation time.

SPEEDY CHUCK BARBECUE

1 arm or blade chuck steak,
  1½ inches thick
instant meat tenderizer
⅔ cup dairy sour cream

⅓ cup barbecue sauce
1 tablespoon instant minced
  onion

Tenderize steak following directions on the package. Combine sour cream, barbecue sauce and onion in a saucepan and heat. Place steak on grill about 4 inches above hot coals and cook for about 30 minutes, turning once. Baste frequently with sauce. Serves 4.

Short ribs make a delightful campsite entrée when they're tenderized and barbecued over coals.

GRILLED SHORT RIBS

6 pounds beef short ribs
instant meat tenderizer
1 8-ounce can tomato sauce
¼ cup cider vinegar
½ cup water
½ teaspoon dry mustard

2½ teaspoons salt
½ teaspoon pepper
1 cup minced onions
1 clove garlic, minced
¼ cup vegetable oil

Sprinkle tenderizer over ribs according to package directions. Remove excess fat, rinse ribs and dry. Combine remaining ingredients in a saucepan and bring to boil; simmer for 10 minutes. Place ribs in shallow pan and cover with cooled sauce; let stand for about 3 hours.

Drain ribs and place on foil-covered grill. Pierce foil at 2-inch intervals so the fat drippings can drain. Grill ribs about 5 inches over coals and cook for about 1 hour, turning and basting frequently. Serves 6 to 8.

Campers probably consume more hamburgers than any other one type of meat. Here are a few favorite "burger" recipes that are easily prepared in camp.

ONION BURGERS

2 pounds ground beef
1 envelope dried onion soup
   mix

½ cup water

Combine all ingredients and shape into 6 to 8 patties, depending on size. Place hamburger patties on grill about 5 inches above coals and cook for about 15 minutes, turning occasionally.

OLD-FASHIONED BURGERS

1½ pounds ground beef
3 tablespoons instant
   minced onion

1 6-ounce can evaporated milk
1½ teaspoons salt
dash pepper
1 to 2 tablespoons steak sauce

Soak onions in milk for several minutes. Combine meat with seasonings, steak sauce and milk–onion mixture. Blend well and shape into five patties. Place patties on grill about 5 inches above hot coals and cook for about 15 minutes, or until done, turning occasionally.

FRANK-BURGERS

1 pound ground beef
6 frankfurters
1 egg, beaten
1 tablespoon Worcestershire
  sauce

¾ teaspoon salt
¾ teaspoon seasoned salt
6 frankfurter buns

Combine ground beef with egg, sauce, and salts. Blend well and press the mixture around each frankfurter. Place Frank-burgers on grill about 5 inches above the coals and cook for about 15 minutes, or until done, turning occasionally. Serve in buns.

PORK AND BEEF BURGERS

1½ pounds ground beef
¾ pound ground pork
2 teaspoons salt
½ teaspoon pepper
1 teaspoon paprika

1 clove garlic, minced
½ cup cold water
¼ cup vegetable oil
sliced onions

Combine beef and pork with salt, pepper, paprika and garlic. Add water; blend well and form into 8 patties. Place hamburgers on grill about 5 inches above coals and grill for about 20 minutes, or until done, turning occasionally. Serve with sliced onions.

For additional hamburger recipes, see Chapter 5, Aluminum Foil Cooking.

CHEESIE BURGERS

1 pound ground beef
1 package spaghetti sauce mix
½ teaspoon salt
1 egg, beaten

¼ pound mozzarella or Swiss
   cheese, sliced
1 tablespoon melted butter or
   margarine

Combine beef, spaghetti sauce mix, salt and egg. Blend well and shape into 2 large patties, each 6 inches in diameter. Place cheese slices on one patty; top with second patty. Press edges together to seal. Brush patty with melted butter or margarine and place on grill about five inches over hot coals. Broil for 10 minutes, turning once, until done. Cut meat in wedges to serve. Makes 3 to 4 servings.

Prepare burgers your favorite way and serve them in buns with a nippy sandwich spread.

CHEESE TOPPERS

½ cup butter or margarine
½ teaspoon dry mustard
¼ teaspoon onion powder

2 tablespoons chopped stuffed
   olives
1 cup Cheddar cheese,
   shredded

Combine butter or margarine with mustard and onion powder; whip until smooth and creamy. Blend in chopped olives and cheese. Spread mixture on cut surfaces of hot split burger buns, fill with burger patty. Makes spread for 12 to 15 sandwiches.

Junior campsite chefs can learn a few lessons in outdoor cookery when you let them prepare these easy-to-fix dishes made with frankfurters.

SPLIT FRANKS

6 frankfurters   6 slices bacon
6 American cheese slices

Split franks lengthwise and stuff with halved cheese slices. Wrap each frank with one slice of bacon and broil on grill about 5 inches over coals until cheese melts and bacon is crisp.

Variations

½ lb. cheddar cheese, grated   ¼ cup pickle relish
¼ cup catsup

Blend above ingredients and stuff split franks with mixture. Grill about 5 inches over coals for about 10 minutes.

Franks can also be basted with any of the barbecue sauces listed earlier in the chapter.

When purchasing spareribs, remember that good quality ribs are pink in color with a generous amount of meat between the rib bones and a thin covering of meat over the bones. Spareribs are juicier and more tender when they're pre-boiled before grilling.

BARBECUE SPARERIBS

4 to 6 pounds spareribs
  (2 sides)
salt and pepper
water
1 cup catsup
½ cup dark corn syrup

½ cup cider vinegar
¼ cup chopped onion
¼ cup Worcestershire sauce
¼ cup prepared mustard
2 teaspoons salt
¼ teaspoon Tabasco

Sprinkle ribs with salt and pepper and place in a large kettle. Add water to cover, bring to boil and simmer covered 1 to 1½ hours, or until ribs are tender. In a saucepan, combine remaining ingredients. Place over heat and bring to boil; reduce heat and simmer about 5 minutes, stirring constantly. Drain ribs and brush with sauce. Place ribs on grill about 6 inches above cooking coals and cook for about 30 minutes, or until browned, turning and basting frequently. Serves 4 to 6.

ONIONED SPARERIBS

6 pounds spareribs
1 10½-ounce can condensed
  cream of mushroom soup
1 10½-ounce can condensed
  onion soup
½ cup catsup

¼ cup salad oil
¼ cup vinegar
2 large cloves garlic, minced
2 tablespoons brown sugar
1 tablespoon Worcestershire
⅛ teaspoon Tabasco sauce

Precook spareribs (see above). Combine remaining ingredients and simmer for about 15 minutes. Drain ribs and brush with sauce. Place on grill about 6 inches above coals. Cook for about 30 minutes, turning and basting frequently. Serves 6.

EASY-DOES-IT RIBS

4 pounds spareribs
1 10½-ounce can condensed
  tomato soup
2 tablespoons soy sauce

2 tablespoons honey
2 tablespoons minced onion
½ teaspoon Worcestershire
¼ teaspoon ginger

Precook ribs (see page 184). Combine soup with remaining ingredients in a saucepan and simmer for about 10 minutes. Drain ribs and brush with sauce. Place ribs on grill about 6 inches above coals and cook for about 30 minutes, turning and basting frequently. Serves 4.

SPICY RIBS

4 pounds spareribs
1 envelope onion soup mix
1 cup catsup
1½ cups water

¼ teaspoon garlic powder
1 teaspoon oregano
1 tablespoon Worcestershire
  sauce

Precook spareribs (see page 184). Combine remaining ingredients in saucepan. Simmer covered for about 10 minutes, stirring frequently. Drain ribs and brush with sauce. Place ribs on grill about 6 inches above coals and cook for about 30 minutes, turning and basting frequently.

For Sweet and Sour spareribs, try this barbecue sauce.

SWEET-SOUR RIBS

¼ cup pineapple juice
⅓ cup soy sauce

1 minced clove garlic
½ teaspoon ground ginger

Combine ingredients and brush on ribs frequently while grilling.

Precooked canned ham is one of our family's favorite campsite dishes. We usually manage to get two meals from a five-pound ham, allowing ½ pound per person, and for variety we slice and grill it over charcoal. We especially enjoy this recipe sent to us by Master Campfire Chef Mrs. Leslie J. Dyer of Orange City, Florida. Mrs. Dyer won Second Prize in the Main Dish category of our recent Open Fire Camp Cooking contest with her entry.

GINGERED HAM

ham slice, 1 inch thick
½ cup ginger ale
½ cup orange juice
¼ cup brown sugar
⅛ teaspoon cloves

1 tablespoon salad oil
1½ teaspoons vinegar
1 teaspoon dry mustard
¼ teaspoon ginger

Blend all ingredients except ham. Place ham in shallow pan and cover with marinade; let stand overnight. Broil ham on grill about 6 inches above coals, turning and brushing frequently with marinade. Cook for about 15 minutes.

This recipe for delicious grilled chicken comes from the unwritten cookbook of my mother-in-law, Mrs. Nalma Adamson, who was an ardent camping enthusiast for many years.

BARBECUED CHICKEN

2 broiling or frying chickens,
  cut up
⅓ cup cider vinegar
1 teaspoon Worcestershire
  sauce
4 tablespoons butter or
  margarine

1 tablespoon tomato paste
½ teaspoon onion salt
¼ teaspoon garlic salt
½ teaspoon salt
⅛ teaspoon pepper
dash paprika

Cut chicken into serving pieces. In saucepan combine vinegar, Worcestershire, butter or margarine and tomato paste with seasonings; heat until butter melts and coat chicken pieces with the mixture. Place chicken on grill about 5 inches above the coals and grill for about 45 minutes, or until tender, basting frequently with sauce. Turn occasionally. Serves 4 to 6.

If your family is a devotee of white meat, you'll enjoy this recipe.

CHICKEN A'ROMA

4 chicken breasts
½ cup butter or margarine

1 envelope Italian-flavor salad
  dressing mix
2 tablespoons lime juice

Melt butter or margarine in saucepan; blend in salad dressing mix and lime juice. Coat chicken breasts with mixture and place skin-side down on grill about 5 inches above coals. Cook for about 45 minutes, basting freqeuntly with sauce. Turn chicken occasionally. Serves 4.

Master Campfire Chef Mrs. Dorothy B. Barrett of Elgin, South Carolina, submitted this recipe for elegant Grilled Trout, and it won First Prize in the Main Dish Category of Our Open Fire Camp Cooking contest.

GRILLED TROUT

8 brook trout, cleaned
2 eggs
1 tablespoon cream
1 teaspoon dried parsley flakes

1 clove garlic, minced
½ teaspoon allspice
8 strips bacon, broiled

Beat eggs, blend with cream, parsley, garlic and allspice. Coat fish inside and out with mixture. Place broiled bacon inside each fish. Lightly oil cooking grill. Place fish on grill about 4 inches above coals, and broil for about 15 minutes, turning once. Serves 8.

Barbecued halibut "Prince Rupert-style" is a good way to prepare Canada's favorite fish.

PRINCE RUPERT HALIBUT

3 small halibut steaks
salt and pepper
paprika

2 tablespoons melted butter or
    margarine
2 tablespoons lemon juice
2 teaspoons salad oil

Season steaks with salt, pepper and paprika. Blend butter or margarine, oil and lemon juice and brush steaks with mixture. Lightly oil the cooking grill and place the fish on grill about 4 inches above cooking coals. Cook for about 10 minutes, turning and basting frequently. Serves 3.

Hawaiian feasts often feature fish wrapped in large leaves and cooked in a pit. Campers can achieve a similar effect by covering the fish with the outer leaves of iceberg lettuce before placing it on a grill. The lettuce provides moisture and prevents the fish from drying out while cooking.

FISH HAWAIIAN

1 or more whole fish, cleaned	onion slices
salt and pepper	iceberg lettuce

Season fish with salt and pepper. Place onion slices inside each body cavity and wrap fish in lettuce leaves. Place on grill about 4 inches over coals and cook for about 10 minutes, turning once.

The next time you enjoy a fine day of fishing, on your way back to camp stop at a country stand and pick up some fresh-picked sweet corn and grill both the fish and the corn over coals.
Prepare your corn first because it takes longer to cook.

GRILLED CORN

Soak sweet corn—with shucks on—in cold water for about one hour. Place the corn on grill about 8 inches above hot cooking coals and grill for about 30 to 40 minutes.

Prepare your fish, and place them on the grill with the corn.

GRILLED FISH

fresh fish	juice of 1 lemon
4 tablespoons butter or margarine	salt and pepper

Melt butter or margarine and add lemon juice. Dress fish and place on grill over coals, basting frequently with lemon–butter and season with salt and pepper. Turn once and cook for about 10 minutes.

What could be simpler than cooking your campsite dinner on a stick? For a culinary treat, here are some easy-to-fix kabob recipes that include main dishes and desserts.

SKEWERED LAMB KABOBS

1 pound lamb, cut into 1½-inch cubes	1 large green pepper, cubed
⅓ cup Italian-style salad dressing	8 small white onions, peeled
	12 cherry tomatoes

Trim fat from lamb and marinate for one hour in salad dressing. Thread lamb cubes on metal skewers, alternating with squares of green pepper and onions. Place tomatoes on separate skewers. Broil lamb and peppers on grill over hot coals for about 15 minutes. Baste frequently with salad dressing, and turn occasionally. Cook skewered tomatoes on grill for 5 minutes. After cooking, place meat and peppers with tomatoes on serving plate. Serve with rice.

SKEWERED LAMB SUPPER

1 pound lamb, cut in 1½-inch
  cubes
¼ cup chopped onion
1 clove garlic, minced
1 teaspoon curry powder
2 tablespoons butter or
  margarine

1 10½-ounce can condensed
  cream of mushroom soup
¼ cup water
1 green pepper, cubed
8 small white onions, peeled
2 apples, quartered

Combine onion, garlic and curry powder with butter or margarine and cook until tender. Add soup and water; cook 5 minutes longer, stirring often. Partially precook green pepper and white onions. On 4 skewers, thread lamb and alternate with apples, green pepper and onions. Place on grill about 5 inches above coals and broil for about 30 minutes, or until meat is tender. Baste kabobs frequently with sauce and turn every five minutes. Serve with remaining sauce. Serves 4.

MARINATED BEEF KABOBS

2 pounds beef, cut into 1-inch
  cubes
4 cups canned pineapple cubes
1 cup pineapple syrup

½ cup soy sauce
1 clove garlic, minced
1 teaspoon ground ginger

Combine syrup, soy sauce, garlic and ginger; blend well. Place beef cubes in shallow pan and cover with marinade; let stand 2 hours. Thread beef cubes on skewers, alternating with pineapple cubes. Broil on grill over coals for about 15 minutes. Baste frequently with marinade and turn occasionally.

QUICK KABOBS

canned luncheon meat
canned whole sweet potatoes
2 cups canned pineapple cubes
½ cup brown sugar

½ cup orange juice
¼ cup vinegar
1 tablespoon mustard

Combine brown sugar, orange juice, vinegar and mustard in saucepan and cook for about 10 minutes. Cut luncheon meat into 1½-inch chunks and thread on skewers, alternating with canned whole sweet potatoes and pineapple cubes. Broil on grill over coals for about 10 minutes, basting frequently with sauce. Turn occasionally.

KABOB FRANKS

frankfurters
bologna slices

dill pickle chunks

Cut franks into 1½-inch cubes. Alternate on skewers with folded bologna slices and dill pickle chunks. Broil on grill over coals for about 10 minutes.

LUSCIOUS PEARS

canned pear halves
canned pineapple rings

maraschino cherries
melted butter or margarine

Place a cherry in the center of each pear half and thread on a skewer. Begin and end skewers with halved pineapple ring. Brush with melted butter or margarine and broil on grill over coals, turning often.

KICKY KABOBS

pound cake   flaked coconut
small can sweetened
   condensed milk

Cut cake into 1½-inch cubes. Dip in milk and roll in flaked coconut. Thread on skewers and broil on grill over very hot coals, turning frequently.

Variation
Dip cake cubes into a mixture of ½ cup honey and 1 tablespoon lemon juice before rolling in coconut. Grill as above.

14
Campsite
Desserts

FEATHER-LIGHT CAKES . . . rich, creamy puddings . . . tangy fruit-filled pies—luscious desserts provide a happy finish to a campsite meal, and when consumed in reasonable quantities, help balance a camper's daily diet by furnishing large amounts of essential nutrients needed for quick energy and vitality.

Campsite dessert should be quick, easy and delicious! Some can be made ahead of time in your kitchen at home; others can be put together quickly at camp.

Among the most refreshing are desserts made from fresh-picked fruits. Serve fresh fruits whole, chilled in your camp cooler, or cooked in puddings, pastries and pies.

Spectacular desserts can be concocted by modifying prepared mixes. Let your imagination run riot with flavorings, fillings, frostings and garnishes.

On leisurely camping days, embellish ordinary campsite meals with rich, delectable desserts made from scratch—the right fillip that will leave your camping family completely satisfied.

On the following pages we've included a wide assortment of delicious and nourishing campsite desserts. Many are quick, savory dishes made from prepared mixes; others are traditional desserts that require more thoughtful preparation. All are de-signed to provide a happy ending to a well-balanced campsite meal.

(Recipes for other campsite desserts may be found in Chapter 5—Aluminum Foil Cooking; Chapter 6—Reflector Oven Cooking; Chapter 7—Dutch Oven Cooking; Chapter 13—Grilling and Barbecuing.)

CAKES

This light, moist cake is especially easy to mix. Serve it warm, topped with prepared whipped cream.

ORANGE NUT CAKE

2 cups biscuit mix	½ teaspoon nutmeg
1 cup chopped walnuts	1 cup milk
2 teaspoons grated orange peel	4 eggs, slightly beaten
2 cups sugar	1 cup salad oil
1½ teaspoons baking powder	¾ cup water
¼ teaspoon salt	
1 teaspoon cinnamon	prepared whipped topping

In large bowl combine biscuit mix, walnuts, 1 teaspoon of grated orange peel, 1 cup of sugar, baking powder, salt, cinnamon and nutmeg. Add milk, eggs and salad oil; stir until well blended. Spoon into greased 9" x 13" baking pan. Bake in 375° F. oven for 30 minutes.

While cake is baking, in saucepan combine the remaining 1 teaspoon orange peel, 1 cup sugar and water. Bring to boil; boil for 2 minutes. Set mixture aside. When cake is done, pour syrup evenly over surface. Cut in squares, topped with prepared whipped topping.

During strawberry season, treat your family to a flavorful cake made with ripe red berries.

STRAWBERRY CRUMBLE

2 cups biscuit mix
¼ cup sugar
1 egg
¾ cup milk
1 cup fresh strawberries,
  cleaned and sliced

TOPPING
½ cup brown sugar
½ cup biscuit mix
¼ cup butter or margarine,
  softened

cream

Combine 2 cups biscuit mix with ¼ cup sugar; stir in 1 egg and ¾ cup milk. Beat vigorously. Pour mixture into greased 9-inch-square pan. Top with sliced strawberries. Combine brown sugar and ½ cup biscuit mix; add softened butter or margarine. Spread crumb topping over strawberries. Bake at 400° F. for 40 minutes. Serve warm with cream.

Blackberry Jam Cake is an old-fashioned dessert that takes quite a bit of preparation time. We've included it in our chapter because it's a light, elegant dessert that provides a delicious finishing touch to a hearty campsite meal.

BLACKBERRY JAM CAKE

1 cup raisins
1 8½ ounce can crushed
  pineapple
1 cup butter or margarine
1 cup sugar

5 eggs
1 cup blackberry jam
2½ cups sifted flour
1 teaspoon baking soda
1 teaspoon cinnamon

1 teaspoon nutmeg
½ teaspoon cloves
⅔ cup buttermilk

1 cup chopped pecans
confectioners' sugar

Soak raisins with pineapple in juice for several hours. Cream butter or margarine and sugar until light and fluffy. Add eggs, one at a time, beating after each addition. Stir in jam. In large bowl, sift together dry ingredients with spices. Add alternately to creamed mixture with buttermilk. Stir in pineapple–raisin mixture and pecans. Pour batter into greased 9″ x 13″ baking pan. Bake in 350° F. oven 50–55 minutes. Dust with sifted confectioners' sugar to serve.

CAKES FROM MIXES

There's a whole new world of dessert mixes on the market that make campsite menu planning easier and more creative. What could be simpler and more foolproof than a cake baked from a package mix? Mixes cut down the list of ingredients that must be toted to camp, and they save the camp chef time-consuming steps in dessert preparation. With them, it's virtually impossible to make a mistake.

For extra-special occasions, transform packaged cake mixes into irresistible desserts by combining them with other flavorful ingredients, as shown in these easy-to-prepare dessert cake recipes.

TASTE OF HONEY CAKE

1 package (2-layer size)
    chocolate cake mix
1 cup chopped pecans

1 6-ounce package semisweet
    chocolate morsels
1 cup honey
½ cup water

Prepare cake mix as directed on package. Add nuts to batter; pour into greased 9" x 13" pan. Scatter chocolate morsels over top. In small pan, combine honey and water; heat to boiling. Pour honey–water mixture over batter; do not mix. Bake at 350° F. for 45 minutes. Serve warm.

APPLESAUCE SPICE CAKE

1 package (2-layer size) spice
   cake mix
½ cup vegetable oil
½ cup brown sugar
4 eggs
½ cup applesauce
⅔ cup water

GLAZE
1 cup confectioners' sugar
2 tablespoons lemon juice

Blend all ingredients except for the glaze in large bowl. Beat until thoroughly blended. Bake in greased, floured 10-inch tube pan at 350° F. for about 45 minutes. Cool right-side up for 25 minutes; remove from pan. Combine confectioners' sugar with lemon juice; drizzle over cooled cake.

LEMON SURPRISE

1 package (2 layer-size) lemon
   cake mix
½ cup sugar
¾ cup vegetable oil
1 cup apricot nectar
4 eggs

GLAZE
1 cup confectioners' sugar
3 tablespoons lemon juice

Combine cake mix with sugar, oil and nectar. Beat well. Add eggs, one at a time, beating after each addition. Bake in greased, floured 10-inch tube pan in 325° F. oven for 1 hour. Make glaze by mixing sugar with lemon juice. Pour glaze over cake while still warm.

DOUBLE LEMON CAKE

1 package (2-layer size) lemon cake mix

1 can lemon pudding confectioners' sugar

Prepare cake mix and bake in 2 9-inch round cake pans as directed on package; remove and cool. Spread 1 layer with lemon pudding; top with second layer. Sprinkle confectioners' sugar over top.

DRESSED-UP HAWAIIAN

1 package (2-layer size) pineapple cake mix

1 10-ounce jar orange marmalade
1 package white frosting mix

Prepare cake mix and bake in 2 9-inch round cake pans as directed on package; remove and cool. Spread 1 layer with orange marmalade; top with second layer. Prepare frosting mix as directed on package; spoon frosting over sides and top of cake.

CHOCOLATE CREAM CAKE

1 package (2-layer size) yellow cake mix
1 can French vanilla pudding

1 can Dutch chocolate pudding

Prepare cake mix and bake in 2 9-inch round cake pans as directed on package; remove and cool. Spread 1 layer with vanilla pudding; top with second layer. Spoon chocolate pudding over top of cake. Serves 6.

Here are several unusual dessert cakes that bake like flavorful, juicy cobblers. They're especially good served warm, topped with marshmallow cream or prepared whipped cream.

CRUNCH CAKE

1 20-ounce can apricot pie
   filling
1 package (1-layer size) white
   cake mix
⅓ cup water

1 egg
½ cup flaked coconut
½ cup chopped pecans
8 tablespoons melted butter
   or margarine

Spread apricot pie filling in bottom of greased 9-inch baking pan. Combine cake mix, water and egg; beat until blended. Pour batter over pie filling; sprinkle with coconut and nuts. Drizzle melted butter or margarine over top. Bake in 350° F. oven 40 minutes.

QUICK APPLE CAKE

1 package (1-layer size) white
   cake mix
1 20-ounce can apple pie
   filling

8 tablespoons melted butter
   or margarine

Spread apple pie filling in bottom of greased 9-inch baking pan. Sprinkle cake mix evenly over apples. Drizzle melted butter or margarine over top. Bake in 350° F. oven for 30 minutes.

Lemon-flavored Gingerbread-Pudding Cake is another tasty campsite dessert made from a packaged mix.

GINGERBREAD-PUDDING CAKE

1 package gingerbread mix	½ cup water
1 15½-ounce can French	2 teaspoons lemon juice
vanilla pudding	1 teaspoon lemon rind

Prepare gingerbread mix as directed on package. Pour into greased 9-inch square baking pan. Combine pudding with water, lemon juice and lemon rind. Spoon mixture over gingerbread. Bake at 350° F. for 45 minutes. Cool at least 30 minutes before serving.

For a simple dessert, add chopped walnuts to gingerbread mix.

WALNUT GINGERBREAD

1 package gingerbread mix	¼ cup sugar
1½ cups chopped walnuts	

Prepare gingerbread mix as directed on package. Stir in 1 cup walnuts. Pour into greased 9-inch square baking pan. Sprinkle with remaining nuts and sugar. Bake at 350° F. for 30 minutes. Serve warm.

PASTRY AND PIES

Preparing a pie crust usually requires a pastry cloth and a rolling pin—two items I never seem to have in my camp pantry. That's why I'm so fond of this recipe for Press-In Butter Pastry—no messy dough-rolling!

PRESS-IN BUTTER PASTRY

¾ cup butter
2 cups unsifted all-purpose
    flour

4 tablespoons sugar
2 egg yolks

Crumble butter into flour and sugar. Stir in egg yolks with fork. Work dough with hands until it forms a smooth ball. Divide in half and press into pie pans. Bake in 325° F. oven for 20 minutes. Makes two 9- or 10-inch single pie crusts.

Fill baked pie shells with canned puddings and top with prepared whipped cream. Or, for a mouth-watering treat, try this recipe for tangy Lemon Chiffon Pie.

LEMON CHIFFON PIE

1 envelope unflavored gelatin
½ cup cold water
1 can lemon pudding

2 egg whites
8-inch pie shell

In saucepan, sprinkle gelatin over cold water. Stir over low heat until gelatin dissolves. Stir gelatin into canned pudding. Beat 2 egg whites until stiff; fold gently into pudding. Pour into 8-inch pie shell. Chill.

On our first camping trip through the south we purchased enough pecans to last all winter. And we also picked up this delicious recipe for Chocolate Pecan Pie.

CHOCOLATE PECAN PIE

3 squares unsweetened chocolate	salt
	4 eggs
3 tablespoons butter or margarine	½ teaspoon vanilla extract
	1½ cups pecan halves
2 cups sugar	10-inch unbaked pie shell
1 tablespoon flour	

In upper section of double boiler, place chocolate and butter or margarine; heat over simmering water, stirring, until butter and chocolate are melted. Combine sugar, flour and salt. In medium-size bowl, beat eggs; stir in sugar and chocolate mixture; blend well. Add vanilla and pecans. Pour mixture into prepared pie shell, bake at 350° F. oven for 35 minutes, or until set. Cool before serving, but don't refrigerate.

Here's another pie that's a favorite of ours. The crust is made from crushed graham crackers.

CHOCOLATE GRAHAM PIE

1 small box graham crackers
(to make 1½ cups crumbs)
¼ cup sugar
½ cup butter or margarine,
melted

6 chocolate bars
1 pint prepared whipped
cream

Crush graham crackers and mix with sugar; stir in melted butter or margarine. Pat mixture firmly into shallow pie pan. Bake in 350° F. oven for 10–15 minutes. Melt chocolate bars in top of double boiler. Blend prepared whipped cream with melted chocolate; spoon mixture into baked pie shell and place in camp cooler for about 4 hours before serving. Serves 8.

Another delicious pie crust can be made from ground Brazil-nut meats. And still another from crushed corn flakes.

CRUSTY CRUST

1 cup corn flakes, crushed
2 tablespoons sugar

⅓ cup melted butter or
margarine

Crush corn flakes and mix with sugar; stir in melted butter or margarine. Pat mixture firmly into shallow pie pan. Fill with canned pudding and top with canned fruit; or fill with sliced fresh fruit and top with prepared whipped topping.

Bake juicy fruit pies using a packaged pie crust mix and

fresh fruit. Pies may be made in dishes of any shape, and some can be made without a bottom crust.

BLACKBERRY PIE

3 cups blackberries, cleaned
1 cup sugar
dash salt

2 tablespoons flour
1 package (2-crust size) pie
    crust mix

In large bowl combine berries with sugar, salt and flour. Prepare pie crust as directed on package. Fill deep dish with fruit mixture. Roll out pie crust dough thicker than usual; cut into strips and crisscross over fruit. Bake in 350° F. oven for 40 minutes.

CHERRY PIE

4 cups cherries, washed and
    pitted
1¼ cups sugar
½ teaspoon nutmeg
2 tablespoons lemon juice

2 tablespoons melted butter
    or margarine
1 package (2-crust size) pie
    crust mix

Combine cherries with sugar, nutmeg, lemon juice and melted butter or margarine. Prepare pie crust according to package directions. Line pie pan with bottom crust; fill with cherry mixture. Cover cherry mixture with top crust; make a few small holes in crust so that steam can escape. Bake at 350° F. for 45 minutes.

Here's a 1-crust strawberry pie that's a refreshing taste treat. Easy to make, too!

STRAWBERRY PIE

½ package (2-crust size) pie
  crust mix
3 cups fresh strawberries,
  cleaned and hulled

½ cup sugar
2 tablespoons cornstarch
dash salt

Prepare single pie crust as directed on package. Bake and cool. Crush 1 cup strawberries, place in saucepan with sugar and cornstarch and cook until thick and syrupy. Fill baked cooled pie shell with remaining 2 cups of berries; cover with hot syrup. Chill and serve.

Pie crust mix can be used to make delicious mini-pies. This recipe for quick mini-pie uses orange marmalade for a filling, but fresh or canned fruit segments could also be used with delightful results.

ORANGE MINI-PIES

1 package (2-crust size) pie
  crust mix
1 12-ounce jar orange
  marmalade

milk
granulated sugar

Make dough as directed on package; divide into 8 parts. On lightly floured surface, roll out each piece into a 5-inch circle. Spoon 1½ tablespoons marmalade on half of each circle, leaving a half-inch edge. Fold other half over marmalade; press edges together to seal. Brush lightly with milk, sprinkle with sugar. Place pies on ungreased cookie sheet; bake in 400° F. oven for 20 minutes. Cool slightly; serves 8.

SKILLET DESSERTS

A large camp skillet is a useful item for cooking eggs, burgers,—or tasty desserts! Here are several recipes for skillet desserts that take little effort to prepare, and they look as delectable as they taste.

The first recipe comes from Master Campfire Chef Mrs. Lilliam M. Lawrence of Terre Haute, Indiana, who won first prize in the dessert category of our 1969 Open Fire Camp Cooking contest with this recipe for Dessert Dumplings, made in a camp skillet.

DESSERT DUMPLINGS

1 cup biscuit mix
1 cup chopped dates
½ cup chopped nuts
1 egg, beaten
¼ cup brown sugar
1 teaspoon vanilla
¼ cup milk

SAUCE
2 cups brown sugar
2 cups water
¼ cup butter

Combine biscuit mix with dates and nuts. In large bowl, beat egg; add brown sugar, vanilla and milk. Stir egg mixture into dry ingredients; blend well.

In large skillet, combine sauce ingredients; heat to boil. Add dumpling batter to sauce by tablespoonfuls. Cover and simmer over low heat for about 25 minutes. Serves 6 to 8.

Fourth prize in the Dessert Category of our 1969 Open Fire Camp Cooking contest was won by Master Campfire Chef Mr. Curtis Humphrey of Glendale, California who entered this recipe for delicious Custard, also made in a camp skillet.

CUSTARD

6 eggs
2 cups sugar
1 cup powdered milk
½ cup water

⅓ cup flour
1 teaspoon vanilla
10 large marshmallows

Beat eggs, place in large skillet. Add remaining ingredients except marshmallows; blend well. Cook over medium heat, stirring constantly, until thick. Add marshmallows and continue cooking until they dissolve. Serves 4 to 6.

Mrs. Herman A. Strasser of Evans, Colorado, won seventh prize in the dessert category of our contest with this recipe for delightful Open Fire Dessert—which can be cooked in a skillet either over a campfire or on a camp stove.

OPEN FIRE DESSERT

1 can sliced peaches, drained
⅓ can water
1 cup sugar
½ teaspoon lemon juice
1 can refrigerator biscuits

4 tablespoons melted butter
   or margarine
¼ cup sugar
cinnamon
cream for serving

Drain peaches. Measure water in empty can; add to drained peaches. Add 1 cup of sugar and lemon juice; pour into large skillet. Place refrigerator biscuits over peaches; brush with melted butter or margarine. Sprinkle with ¼ cup sugar, cinnamon. Cover and simmer for about 20 minutes. Serve warm with cream. Apricots, canned cherries or pineapple may also be used.

Quick Blueberry Skillet Dessert won tenth prize in the dessert category of our Open Fire Camp Cooking contest for Mrs. John Bonebright of Chinook, Montana. The dessert has since become one of our family's favorites.

QUICK BLUEBERRY SKILLET DESSERT

1 13½-ounce package
  blueberry muffin mix
1 egg
⅔ cup milk

¼ cup sugar
3 tablespoons butter or
  margarine
confectioners' sugar

Prepare blueberry muffin mix according to package directions, using egg and milk. Add sugar to batter; blend well. Heat 2 tablespoons butter in skillet; pour in batter. Cover and cook over medium heat until brown around edges. Turn over onto large plate. Melt remaining tablespoon butter or margarine in skillet. Slip dessert back into skillet over melted butter, continue cooking for about 5 more minutes. Serve warm with confectioners' sugar dusted over top.

Easy-to-prepare Banana Shortcake won twelfth prize in the dessert category of our Open Fire Camp Cooking con-

test. The recipe was submitted by Master Campfire Chef Mrs. Quinten R. Graham of Akron, Ohio.

BANANA SHORTCAKE

¼ cup butter or margarine
2 or 3 bananas, peeled and
  quartered
2 tablespoons lemon juice
⅔ cup brown sugar

¼ teaspoon cinnamon
pound cake, sliced into 4
  1-inch slices
marshmallow cream

Melt butter or margarine in skillet; add bananas and sprinkle with lemon juice, brown sugar and cinnamon. Spoon liquid over bananas, basting frequently. Place bananas on sliced cake, top with syrup and marshmallow cream topping. Serves 4.

QUICK TRICKS

Here's a collection of brief but delicious campsite desserts that make use of canned and ready-to-go packaged foods.

LEMON WHIP

1 cup whipped topping
1 can lemon pudding

flaked coconut
red currant jelly

Fold whipped topping into pudding; stir until well blended. Spoon into 6 serving dishes. Sprinkle coconut on top and garnish with small spoonful of jelly. Serves 6.

DUTCH RICE PUDDING

1 can rice pudding

1 can Dutch chocolate
  pudding

Combine puddings; spoon into dessert dishes. Garnish with whipped topping and chocolate sprinkles, if desired. Serves 6.

SNAPPY PUDDING

1 large can fruit cocktail,
  drained

1 can vanilla pudding

Stir drained fruit into pudding. Chill; top with whipped topping, if desired. Serves 6 to 8.

PINEAPPLE-PECAN TREATS

1 1-pound can pecan nut cake
1 tablespoon butter or
  margarine

½ cup pineapple preserves

Cut cake into 12 slices. In heavy skillet, melt butter or margarine; brown cake slices on both sides. Spread half the slices with about 1½ tablespoons pineapple preserves; top with remaining slices. Serves 6.

CHERRY GEMS

1 ready-baked pound cake
  (about 12 ounces)

1 1-pound can cherry pie
  filling

Cut pound cake into 12 slices. Cover 6 slices with cherry pie filling. Top with remaining cake slices. Spoon on remaining pie filling. Serves 6.

DATE-NUT DESSERT

1 can date-and-nut roll
1 can mandarin orange
  segments

whipped topping

Divide date-nut roll into six pieces. Place each piece on a dessert plate; top with orange segments. Garnish with prepared whipped topping; add toasted almonds, if desired. Serves 6

FRUIT CUP

3 sliced apricots
1 cup seedless grapes
1 cup blueberries, cleaned

½ cup sugar
¼ cup water
mint sprigs

Combine apricots, grapes and blueberries in large bowl. In saucepan, heat sugar, water and a few mint sprigs. Stir until sugar is dissolved. Strain sugar–water mixture over fruit; chill Garnish with mint sprigs. Serves 4.

FRUIT SUPREME

1 1-pound can sliced peaches
1 8-ounce can pineapple
  tidbits
½ cup chopped nuts

1 cup dairy sour cream
¼ cup brown sugar
pound cake slices

Drain fruit; combine and place in aluminum pie pan. Sprinkle with nuts, cover with sour cream and sprinkle with brown sugar. Place under broiler until bubbly. Serve sauce on pound cake slices. Serves 4 to 6.

POACHED PEARS

2 pears
1 7-ounce bottle ginger ale

1 stick cinnamon

Halve pears; peel and core. Place cored-side down in skillet; add ginger ale and cinnamon. Cover, simmer 10 minutes, or until tender. Remove cinnamon stick; chill. Serves 4.

CHILLED APPLE DESSERT

1 can apple slices, chilled
2 tablespoons butter or
  margarine

1 tablespoon brown sugar
½ teaspoon cinnamon
1 cup crushed corn flakes

Divide canned apple slices into 4 dessert dishes. In saucepan, melt butter or margarine; add brown sugar, cinnamon and crushed corn flakes. Spread mixture over apple slices. Serve with cream. Serves 4.

CINNAMON APPLES

4 apples
2 cups water
1 cup sugar

6 tablespoons lemon juice
2 tablespoons red cinnamon
  candies

Peel, core and slice apples. Place apple slices in heavy skillet. Add water, sugar and lemon juice. Simmer until apples are tender. Add 2 tablespoons red cinnamon candies; stir until candies are dissolved. Serve warm. Serves 4.

FRIED APPLES

2 cooking apples
brown sugar

4 tablespoons butter or
 margarine
cinnamon

Peel, core and cut apples into ½-inch slices. Sprinkle slices lightly with brown sugar. Melt butter or margarine in skillet; sauté apple slices until tender. Dust with cinnamon. Serves 4 to 6.

ELEGANT APPLESAUCE

2 cups unsweetened
 applesauce
4 tablespoons raisins

dash cinnamon
4 teaspoons chopped walnuts

Combine applesauce with raisins and cinnamon; heat; stir often. Serve warm; sprinkle with chopped walnuts. Serves 4.

UPSIDE-DOWN SHORTCAKE

4 tablespoons butter or
 margarine
½ cup light brown sugar
6 packaged individual sponge
 shortcakes

1 10-ounce can pineapple
 slices, drained
whipped topping
6 maraschino cherries
 (optional)

Melt butter or margarine and sugar in skillet. Add pineapple slices and heat through. Place shortcakes on dessert dishes. Place pineapple slice on each shortcake, top with margarine–sugar mixture. Garnish with whipped topping and cherries, if desired. Serves 6.

PEACH MELBA SHORTCAKE

1 can refrigerator biscuits	1 tablespoon cornstarch
cinnamon sugar	¼ cup cold water
1 can raspberries	12 fresh peach halves

Flatten biscuits until about ⅜ inch thick. Place on baking sheet and sprinkle with cinnamon sugar. Bake according to package directions. In saucepan, heat raspberries and cornstarch, stirring constantly. Place a baked biscuit on dessert dish. Top with 2 peach halves, cover wtih warm raspberry sauce. Serves 6.

15
Campfire
Snacks

THE CAMPSITE CHEF can't get away with serving just three hearty meals a day! Big eaters become ravenous in the great outdoors and demand food between meals as well.

An interesting variety of appetizing snacks can be made by combining foods found in the four basic food groups—milk and dairy products, meat, fruits and vegetables and breads and cereals—and these nutritious treats are helpful in balancing the day's total intake of food.

Calorie-conscious campers should snack on raw or cooked fruits and vegetables, clear soups or artificially sweetened fruit juices and carbonated beverages. Coffee and tea, artificially sweetened, of course, can also be enjoyed in quantity.

For campers who aren't watching their weight, here are some suggestions for healthful, delicious snacks—some heated over a campfire and others made in your camp kitchen.

CEREAL SNACKS

Satisfy between-meal hunger by serving nutritious snacks with cold cereal as a principal ingredient. The following cereal snacks can be prepared either by cooking over a campfire in a disposable foil pan or by heating in your galley oven.

NIBBLER'S DELIGHT

½ cup butter or margarine
½ teaspoon garlic powder
¼ teaspoon onion salt
½ teaspoon Worcestershire
  sauce
3 cups puffed wheat

3 cups puffed rice
1 6½-ounce can salted
  peanuts
½ cup Parmesan cheese,
  grated

Put butter or margarine in disposable foil pan; heat over campfire until melted. Stir in garlic powder, onion salt and Worcestershire sauce. Add puffed wheat, puffed rice and peanuts, tossing lightly to combine. Cook over campfire for an additional 45 minutes, stirring occasionally. Stir in Parmesan cheese; cook an additonal 15 minutes. Makes 8 cups of mix.

CAMPFIRE PARTY MIX

6 tablespoons butter or
  margarine
4 teaspoons Worcestershire
  sauce
½ teaspoon garlic powder

6 cups of Chex cereal (corn,
  wheat and rice, mixed as
  desired)
1 jar dry roasted peanuts

Melt butter or margarine in disposable foil pan, heated over campfire. Stir in Worcestershire and garlic powder. Add cereals and peanuts; mix until all pieces are coated. Heat over campfire about 45 minutes, stirring occasionally. Spread on absorbent paper to cool. Makes 8 cups of mix.

CHOCOLATE MUNCHERS

1 cup sugar-coated ready-to-eat cereal

1 cup raisins

1 cup semisweet chocolate morsels

1 cup salted peanuts

Combine all ingredients and serve.

BUTTERSCOTCH MUNCHERS

1 cup butterscotch morsels

1 cup broken corn chips

1 cup potato sticks

1 cup broken pretzel sticks

1 cup presweetened ready-to-eat cereal

Combine all ingredients and serve.

FRUIT AND VEGETABLE SNACKS

Raw or cooked, vitamin-rich fruits and vegetables make refreshing snacks. Carrots, celery, apples, bananas, dates, grapes, oranges, peaches, pears and raisins are all natural foods that supply quick energy without spoiling appetites.

Peanuts, which are actually beans and not nuts, are another quick-energy snack and an excellent source of protein. Eaten out of hand or mixed with other snack foods like raisins, the peanut is still the most economical nut available—and one of the most delicious.

For easy campsite snacks, serve your family a combination of fruits and vegetables, and for variety, include snacks of cheese, ice cream and other dairy products.

For a simple snack, combine an apple with cheddar cheese.

CHEESE-APPLES

1 apple   1 slice Cheddar cheese

Core apple; cut into 4 slices, crosswise. Spread 2 apple slices each with ½ slice of Cheddar cheese. Make sandwiches by covering with remaining 2 apple slices. Serves 1.

Apples can be prepared in a number of ways. Here are several recipes that are easy to prepare, but mmmmmm—how delicious!

CAMPFIRE APPLES

1 apple   sugar
melted butter or margarine

Core apple; cut into ½-inch slices. Brush slices with melted butter or margarine; grill over campfire in hinged broiler 3 to 4 minutes on each side, or until brown and tender. Sprinkle with sugar and serve warm.

SUGAR APPLES

apples   brown sugar

Spear apple with green stick and roast over campfire until skin cracks. Peel skin from apple and roll peeled apple in brown sugar. Roast again over fire until sugar melts. Cool slightly before eating.

CARAMEL APPLES

½ pound caramels   apples

Melt caramels in saucepan over low flame. Spear apples on short stick and spin in melted caramel syrup to coat. Cool slightly before eating.

MEAT SNACKS

Canned corned beef is a versatile meat dish that often appears as a main course entrée. Here we've used canned corned beef as the basis for an appetizing spread served with vegetables, crackers or bread.

CORNED BEEF SPREAD

1 12-ounce can corned beef
1 8-ounce package cream
  cheese, softened

3 tablespoons prepared
  horseradish
2 tablespoons minced onion
dash pepper

In large bowl, combine all ingredients. Blend well; cover and chill until needed. Makes about 2½ cups spread.

For snacks

Wash and cut celery stalks in short lengths; stuff with meat spread.

Wash cherry tomatoes; cut out centers, drain; stuff with meat spread.

Melba toast, snack crackers or breads may also be spread with meat mixture for delicious appetizers or snacks. Garnish with slice of ripe olive or pimiento-stuffed olive, if desired.

Other meat snacks can be prepared using canned Vienna sausage or canned cocktail franks heated over a campfire, served hot with crackers or bread. Luncheon meat makes a delicious inexpensive meat snack—try this recipe for Bologna Rol-ups.

BOLOGNA ROLL-UPS

12 bologna slices
1 8-ounce package cream
  cheese

⅓ cup sweet pickle relish,
  drained

Blend softened cream cheese with drained pickle relish. Spread on 12 bologna slices; roll up. Makes 12 rolls.

For a hot meat treat, try this recipe for Bacon Rolls.

BACON ROLLS

8 strips bacon

4 tablespoons peanut butter

Spread slices of uncooked bacon with peanut butter. Roll up tightly and fasten with toothpick. Grill over campfire until crisp.

Variations

Cut stuffed olives into halves, put together with cheese spread; roll up on uncooked bacon, wrap and grill.

Roll ½-inch cube of Cheddar cheese in bacon; wrap and grill.

Roll large pickled onion in ½-slice bacon; wrap and grill.

PARTY DIPS

Party dips turn corn chips, potato chips or crackers into delicious snacking any time of day. Some of the easiest dips to prepare are those made by blending one envelope of dried soup mix with one pint of sour cream. For variety, try this dip made with soup.

CAMP PARTY DIP

1 10½-ounce can condensed
   bean with bacon soup
¼ cup chili sauce

1 teaspoon minced onion
1 teaspoon Worcestershire
   sauce

Blend above ingredients. Chill. Makes about 1½ cups of dip.

For an exotic dip, try this calorie-loaded Avocado–Crab mixture.

AVOCADO-CRAB TREAT

1 7½-ounce can crab meat,
  flaked
1 avocado, mashed

½ cup sour cream
½ teaspoon salt

Blend above ingredients; chill before serving.

SNACKS-ON-A-STICK

An endless variety of snacks can be cooked on a stick over a campfire. Here are just a few recipes to add to your own list of favorites.

S'MORES

2 graham crackers
1 marshmallow

4 squares milk chocolate

Roast marshmallow on stick until golden brown. Place on graham cracker, cover with chocolate squares; top with remaining graham cracker. One delicious serving.

MORE S'MORES

1 marshmallow

1 square milk chocolate

Insert chocolate square into marshmallow. Cook on stick over campfire until brown. One very rich serving.

PEANUT BUTTER S'MORES

2 graham crackers
1 marshmallow

peanut butter

Roast marshmallow on stick until golden brown. Spread 1 cracker with peanut butter; cover with roasted marshmallow; top with remaining cracker. Very sticky serving for 1.

We could go on and on with more S'Mores. There's an infinite number of ways to prepare them—all delicious, all sticky and all beloved by youngsters everywhere.

Instead, let's proceed to a more sophisticated stick cooking recipe that was entered in our 1969 Open Fire Camp Cooking contest. Master Campfire Chef Mrs. Dolores W. Thomas, of Columbus, Ohio, won ninth prize in the dessert category of our contest with this recipe for Cherry Shortcake Doughboys, cooked on a stick over a campfire.

CHERRY SHORTCAKE DOUGHBOYS

1 1-pound 6-ounce can cherry
pie filling

1 can refrigerator biscuits

Heat filling in saucepan. Separate biscuits, flatten and mold one biscuit around end of green stick. Toast over hot coals. When brown, slip dough off stick and fill with warm cherry filling.

Variations

Fill cooked biscuit twists with your choice of jam, jelly or preserves.

For a hearty snack, wrap unbaked biscuits around cube of steak. Mold around end of green stick and toast over hot coals.

Legions of Girl Scouts and Campfire Girls have perfected the following stick cooking recipes.

MOCK ANGEL CAKE

stale bread   flaked coconut
condensed milk

Trim crusts from bread; cut into 2-inch squares. Spear bread squares on cooking stick, dip into condensed milk and then into flaked coconut. Toast over hot coals until brown.

SUGAR CAKES

stale bread   cinnamon sugar
melted butter or margarine

Trim crusts from bread; cut into 2-inch squares. Spear bread squares on cooking stick, dip into melted butter or margarine and then into cinnamon sugar mixture. Toast over hot coals until crisp.

HAIRY SQUARES

stale bread   flaked coconut
maple syrup

Trim crusts from bread; cut into 2-inch squares. Spear bread squares on cooking stick, dip into syrup and then into flaked coconut. Toast over hot coals until crisp.

CANDY

Candy making is a cooking technique easily mastered by junior campfire chefs, with senior chef looking on, of course. Here's a collection of easy-to-fix candies that young-sters enjoy making—delicious tidbits for eating around an evening campfire.

SHORTCUT FUDGE

1 12-ounce package semisweet   1 tablespoon water
  chocolate morsels   1 teaspoon vanilla flavoring
⅔ cup sweetened condensed
  milk

In saucepan, melt chocolate morsels over low heat, stirring constantly. Remove from heat and stir in remaining ingredients; blend until smooth. Pour into greased 5″ x 10″ pan. Cool until firm; cut into 1-inch squares.

Variations

Shape 1-inch squares into round patties; dip into colored candy sprinkles.

Shape 1-inch squares into oval patties; place pecan half in center of each.

Cut into 2-x-½-inch rectangles; dip one end into flaked coconut.

MARSHMALLOW CREAM FUDGE

1 10-ounce jar marshmallow cream
⅔ cup evaporated milk
¼ cup butter
1½ cups sugar

¼ teaspoon salt
1 12-ounce package semisweet chocolate mint morsels
1 teaspoon vanilla extract

In large saucepan, combine marshmallow cream, milk, butter, sugar and salt. Place over medium heat; bring to full boil. Boil 5 minutes, stirring constantly. Remove from heat; add chocolate mint morsels and vanilla. Stir until smooth. Pour into greased 8″ x 8″ pan. Cool until firm. Cut into 2-inch squares. Garnish with flaked coconut, candied cherries or pineapple chunks.

PEANUT BUTTER FUDGE

1 pint marshmallow cream
1 cup chunky peanut butter
1 teaspoon vanilla

2 cups sugar
⅔ cup milk

Combine marshmallow, peanut butter and vanilla in large mixing bowl. In saucepan, combine sugar and milk; cook over medium heat to soft-ball stage. Pour sugar–milk mixture over peanut butter mixture and stir until mixed. Pour mixture into greased 8-inch square pan. Cool; cut into 1-inch squares.

RAISIN-NUT TREAT

1 6-ounce package semisweet
  chocolate morsels
1 cup raisins

1 cup peanuts
¼ cup light corn syrup
1 tablespoon water

Combine chocolate morsels, corn syrup and water; cook over low heat until chocolate is melted. Remove; divide mixture in half. Stir raisins into one half, peanuts into the other. Drop by spoonfuls on waxed paper. Cool until firm. Makes 3 dozen treats.

QUICKIE SWEET

1 12-ounce package semisweet
  chocolate morsels

1 tablespoon butter or
  margarine
1½ cup chopped walnuts

Melt chocolate morsels over medium low heat; add butter or margarine and cook until melted. Remove from heat and add chopped nuts. Drop by spoonfuls on waxed paper. Cool until firm.

Buttery flavored popcorn will never take the place of milk or meat, but it is a delicious campfire snack that everyone enjoys. Vary the taste of popcorn by adding garlic salt, seasoned salt or grated Parmesan cheese. To make colored popcorn, follow this recipe:

COLORFUL SUGAR CORN

2 cups sugar
1 cup light corn syrup
1 cup water

½ cup butter or margarine
2 quarts of popped corn
your choice of food coloring

Combine ingredients in saucepan and cook to soft-crack stage (260° F.). Stir in your choice of food coloring. Pour colored syrup over 2 quarts of popped corn and mix thoroughly. Press coated popcorn into shapes or spread on cookie sheet to dry, then break apart.

PIE IRON COOKING

Long-handled cast-iron disks, hinged at one side, were first used by 16th-century chefs to bake waffles and other flat breads in a kitchen fireplace. Those early disks were the forerunners of our modern-day camper pie iron—a handy outdoor cooking utensil that campers use to bake pies, hot sandwiches and even pizza.

We own three aluminum pie irons and they all show signs of heavy wear. We use them to create filling and delicious camp-fire snacks and find they're surprisingly easy to use.

Before you cook with a pie iron, heat it over hot coals. Then, for each serving, spread one slice of bread with butter and lay buttered side down on one side of hot iron. Spoon one or two spoonfuls of filling on top of bread. Butter another slice of bread and lay buttered side up over filling. Close mold, trim crusts and place iron over hot coals for about 5 minutes, turning from time to time. Pies are done when bread is golden brown.

Following the directions for pie iron cooking, create juicy fruit pies by spooning your choice of canned pie filling between the two slices of bread. For heartier fare, try these recipes for nourishing campfire snacks.

PIE IRON GRILLED CHEESE

Heat iron; prepare bread. Place one slice of American cheese between bread slices. Close, trim and cook for about 5 minutes over hot coals, turning occasionally.

PIE IRON STEW

Heat iron; prepare bread. Spoon canned chicken á la king between bread slices. Close mold, trim and cook for about 5 minutes over hot coals, turning occasionally.

Variation

Spoon canned beef stew between bread slices and cook as above.

PIE IRON PIZZA

Heat iron; prepare bread. Place spoonful of canned pizza sauce on first slice of bread. Top with shredded mozzarella cheese. Sprinkle with oregano. Cover with second slice of bread, close mold and trim. Cook over hot coals for about 5 minutes, turning occasionally.

16
Beverages

STRENUOUS OUTDOOR exercise uses up more body moisture than most campers realize. Avert dehydration by serving your family plenty of nourishing, refreshing beverages.

In camp, beverages can be categorized in two main groups—hot and cold. Hot drinks served in mugs or cups are ideal chill-chasers when you're camping in frosty cool weather. Cold drinks are refreshing anytime, but they're especially appealing on hot sultry summer days.

Satisfy your family's thirst and replenish their bodies' supply of liquid with these suggestions for nutritious hot and cold beverages. They're quick and easy to prepare—and guaranteed to be delicious!

COLD DRINKS

The most perfect campsite beverage is milk. It contains protein, fat and carbohydrates as well as essential vitamins and minerals. Children and teen-agers are encouraged to drink three or four glasses daily; adults need two or more glasses, or the equivalent in milkmade foods.

Served ice cold, milk is a delicious thirst quencher by itself. To give it a surprisingly new taste, however, whip up tall, frosty drinks that combine milk with other flavorful ingredients.

PEANUT BUTTER DELIGHT

3½ cups milk
4 tablespoons honey

4 tablespoons creamy peanut butter

In mixing bowl, blend honey with peanut butter, using egg beater. Gradually add milk, ½ cup at a time. After all the milk is added, beat for an extra minute. Pour into glasses. Serves 4.

ALL SHOOK UP

½ cup milk
4 eggs

8 tablespoons orange marmalade
6 tablespoons lime syrup

In mixing bowl, beat eggs thoroughly. Then add remaining ingredients and beat again. Pour into glasses. Serves 4.

CHOCO-MINT MILK

4 cups milk
1 cup chocolate syrup

1 teaspoon peppermint extract

Stir syrup and extract into milk. Serves 4.

CHOCO-CHERRY MILK

4 cups milk
1 cup chocolate syrup

2 teaspoons cherry extract

Stir syrup and extract into milk. Serves 4.

CAMP MILK SHAKE

1 can Dutch chocolate
pudding, chilled

3 cups milk

In large jar, combine milk with pudding. Cover and shake, blending until smooth and frothy. Pour into 4 glasses.

If the refrigerator in your camping rig is equipped with a small freezer, carry sherbet or ice cream for a special campsite treat. Here are three delightful, refreshing coolers made by combining milk with ice cream or sherbet.

GROOVY MILK

1 pint lemon sherbet
1 quart cold milk

few drops vanilla extract

Place sherbet in large pitcher and soften with spoon. Blend in milk and stir until thoroughly combined. Add vanilla, beat until well blended. Pour into serving glasses. Serves 4 to 6.

FROTHY MILK DELIGHT

1 small can evaporated milk   1 pint lemon sherbet
1 quart ginger ale

Pour milk into large pitcher. Slowly add ginger ale, stirring. Add sherbet and blend well. Pour into serving glasses. Serves 4 to 6.

KATE'S MILK COOLER

2 tablespoons milk   1 scoop ice cream
2 tablespoons chocolate syrup   plain soda water

In large glass, place milk and syrup. Stir with spoon until blended. Add 1 scoop ice cream. Fill to brim with plain soda water. A campsite soda for 1.

PEPPERMINT MILK

1 quart milk   6 peppermint candy sticks
4 ¾-ounce envelopes   marshmallow topping
  chocolate-flavored
  milk-shake mix

In large jar, combine 2 cups milk and 2 envelopes milk-shake mix. Cover and shake, blending well. Pour into pitcher. Repeat process for remaining milk and milk-shake mix. Pour into 6 glasses. Place candy stick in each glass; top with spoonful of marshmallow topping. Serves 6.

Breakfast beverages made from citrus fruits are rich in vitamins and minerals and help balance a camper's daily diet. Serve refreshing beverages made from powdered juice crystals or condensed fruit juices. Or, for a delightful change, try Orange Nog by combining an instant breakfast drink with milk.

ORANGE NOG

1 cup cold milk
3 teaspoons instant breakfast
   orange drink

1 egg, separated
nutmeg (optional)

Place milk in tall glass. Add 2 teaspoons instant breakfast drink to milk and beat. Add egg yolk and blend well. In mixing bowl, beat egg white until foamy. Add remaining teaspoon instant breakfast drink and continue beating until stiff. Spoon egg-white mixture over milk mixture. Sprinkle with nutmeg if desired. Serves 1.

A carbonated soft drink chilled in a camp cooler is an easy way to satisfy a giant thirst. For a more nourishing drink, create your own frosty coolers by blending fruit juices with syrups, soft drinks or other tangy ingredients.

ORANGE NIP

2 cups orange juice
½ cup lemon juice
½ cup pineapple juice

2 cups water
1 cup ginger ale
sugar, to taste

In large bowl, mix all ingredients except sugar. Add sugar, one tablespoon at a time, until the mixture is sweet enough. Pour mixture into juice container, chill. Serves 6 to 8.

PURPLE POTION

1½ cups lemon juice
1½ cups grape juice
1 egg

sugar, to taste
plain soda water

In large glass jar, combine all ingredients except sugar and soda. Cover and shake, blending well. Add sugar to taste. Pour equal amounts into four glasses. Fill each glass to the brim with plain soda water. Serves 4.

RASPBERRY ROYAL

½ package raspberry-flavored
   drink powder
½ package grape-flavored
   drink powder
4 cups water

¾ cup sugar
½ cup orange juice
¼ cup lemon juice
½ cup crushed pineapple

In large pitcher, dissolve drink powders in water. Add sugar, fruit juices and pineapple; chill. Serves 8 to 10.

GRAPE FIZZ

1 46-ounce can grape drink
1 12-ounce can carbonated
   lemon–lime drink

1 12-ounce can ginger ale

Combine grape drink with lemon–lime drink and ginger ale; blend well. Chill. Serves 8 to 10.

QUICK ORANGE COOLER

1 18-ounce can orange–apricot   2 tablespoons lemon juice
  juice

Combine ingredients in large pitcher. Serve in small glasses, garnished with fresh mint, if desired. Serves 6.

QUICK LEMON-MINT TEA

1 envelope lemon-flavored   1 envelope mint-flavored
  iced tea mix   iced tea mix
                              4 cups water

In large pitcher, combine tea mixes. Add water and blend until mixes are dissolved. Pour over ice in 6 tall glasses. Serves 6.

HAWAIIAN LIME COOLER

1 6-ounce can frozen   2 6-ounce cans frozen
  concentrate red Hawaiian   concentrate lemonade
  punch   12 cups water

In large pitcher, combine Hawaiian punch with lemonade. Add water and blend until dissolved. Chill. Serves 10 to 12.

FRUIT SPARKLER

6 cups chilled canned apple   6 cups chilled canned
  juice   orange-grapefruit juice

In large pitcher, combine juices, blending well. Serves 10 to 12.

SLOW SIPPER

1 12-ounce can chilled V-8 juice

¼ cup chilled apple juice

Combine juices, chill. Serves 2 to 3.

CHERRY-ALE

4 cups orange juice
½ cup maraschino cherry syrup

1 cup ginger ale

Combine above ingredients, blending well. Chill in camp cooler. Serves 4.

CAROL'S PUNCH

2 cans frozen lemonade concentrate

½ quart cherry juice
½ quart apricot juice

Reconstitute lemonade following directions on can. Add cherry juice and apricot juice. Chill. Serves 10.

Dip into your rig's freezer for raspberry sherbet and please the youngsters with this delightful beverage.

RASPBERRY COOLER

1 pint raspberry sherbet, softened

1 12-ounce bottle lemon–lime soda

In large pitcher, blend softened sherbet with soda. Pour into 4 glasses. Serves 4.

ORANGE PICK-ME-UP

1 7-ounce jar orange-flavored
    instant breakfast drink
5 cups water

2 cups cranberry juice
2 cups ginger ale

Combine breakfast drink with water and cranberry juice. Blend well and chill. Add ginger ale when ready to serve. Serves 10 to 12.

CAMP LEMONADE

1 cup bottled lemon juice
1 cup sugar

6 cups water
strawberries

Combine lemon juice with sugar and water. Blend well and chill. (Add more sugar if desired.) Wash and hull berries; slice. Pour chilled juice into glasses and garnish with sliced berries. Serves 10 to 12.

LEMONADE-TEA

1½ cups boiling water
3 tea bags or 1 tablespoon
    loose tea
½ teaspoon whole cloves
1 stick cinnamon

1 cup sugar
1 cup bottled lemon juice
2 teaspoons grated lemon rind
cold water

Pour boiling water over tea and spices. Steep 5 minutes and

strain. Add sugar; stir until dissolved. Add lemon juice and rind. Store in covered container in refrigerator. For individual servings, pour ⅓ cup syrup over ice in tall glasses; fill with cold water. Stir briskly.

APPLE JUICE 'N' TEA

2 cups chilled apple juice   2 cups strong tea

Combine apple juice with tea. Pour over ice into tall glasses, garnish with lemon slice if desired. Serves 5 to 6.

For offbeat summer refreshment, try these cooling beverages made by combining soup with fruit or vegetable juice.

ENERGY COCKTAIL

1 10½-ounce can condensed   ½ soup can water
   beef broth   1 12-ounce can V-8 juice

Combine all ingredients, blend well and chill. Serves 5.

BEEFED-UP JUICE

2 cans condensed beef broth   6 tablespoons lemon juice
½ soup can water

Combine ingredients, blend well and chill. Serves 6.

Hot Drinks

In camp, many good conversations and friendships begin over mugs of steaming hot coffee. In fact, many campers even fly a "coffee flag" as a gesture of camping hospitality. A coffee flag is simply a small piece of cloth with a drawing of a coffee pot stitched or stenciled on one side. When you see one flying at a campsite, it's your invitation to come on over for a cup of fresh-perked brew and a friendly handshake.

Whether you fly a coffee flag or just plan to host a crowd of campers, the easiest way to brew a large quantity of coffee is to camp next to an electrical outlet and rent or borrow a commercial-size electric coffee percolator.

Without electricity, you can still brew a large quantity of hearty coffee by making it in a two-gallon kettle and heating it over a campfire. The following recipe for Campfire Coffee serves 40, and it can be made in two ways:

CAMPFIRE COFFEE

1 pound regular grind coffee   2 gallons water
large kettle   cheesecloth bag and strings

Boiling method

Place water in kettle and heat over campfire. Bring water to boil. Place coffee in cheesecloth bag, tie and drop bag in boiling water. Boil for about 8 minutes, remove bag and serve hot. Makes 40 cups.

Cold water method

Place water in kettle. Place coffee in cheesecloth bag, tie and drop in water. Place kettle over campfire and bring water to boil. Boil three minutes—or longer for a stronger brew. Remove bag and serve hot. Makes 40 cups.

If you're getting together with a few camping friends, here's a recipe for a quick coffee with a tangy chocolate flavor.

CO-COFFEE

2 cups water
2 cups milk
4 tablespoons instant coffee

4 tablespoons instant
   chocolate-flavored mix

Combine water and milk in saucepan, bring to boil. Add instant coffee and instant chocolate mix; stir until dissolved. Serve hot. Serves 4.

Coffee Cocoa can also be made with freeze-dried coffee powder:

COFFEE COCOA

1 tablespoon instant cocoa mix
2 teaspoons freeze-dried
  coffee powder

¾ cup milk, scalded
2 tablespoons thawed frozen
  whipped topping

Place cocoa mix and coffee in large coffee mug. Stir in scalded milk. Continue stirring until mixes are dissolved. Top with prepared whipped topping. Serves 1.

Cocoa is always a favorite with the younger set. Here are several ways to serve creamy rich cocoa.

CAMPFIRE COCOA

10 cups water
3 cups instant cocoa mix

3 cans evaporated milk

Place water in large kettle. Heat over campfire and bring to boil. Add instant cocoa mix, heat and stir until dissolved. Remove from fire. Add evaporated milk, stir until well blended. Return to fire, heat through. Serve hot. Serves 10 to 12.

MATE'S COCOA

⅓ cup instant nondairy coffee creamer
⅓ cup cocoa
⅓ cup sugar

dash salt
1 cup water
4½ cups milk

In large saucepan, combine coffee creamer, cocoa, sugar and salt. Slowly stir in water. Bring to boil; simmer and stir for about 2 minutes. Stir in milk and heat to serving temperature. Serve hot. Serves 6.

For an extrarich chocolate beverage, prepare this unusual recipe on your camp stove.

CHOCOLATE IMPERIAL

4 cups milk
1 tablespoon sugar, or to taste
1 teaspoon vanilla extract
pinch of salt

2 ounces semisweet chocolate, melted
2 egg yolks
1 tablespoon cold water

In large saucepan, combine milk, sugar, vanilla and salt. Scald without boiling. Beat melted chocolate into scalded milk. Beat egg yolks with 1 tablespoon cold water. Remove chocolate milk from heat and gradually pour a small amount of it into egg yolks, beating constantly. Pour egg mixture back into remaining chocolate, beating constantly. Heat but don't boil. Makes 4 cups of rich chocolate.

On a chilly evening, when you're sitting around a campfire, delight the youngsters by serving delicious beverages heated over the fire. Here are two spicy drinks most children adore—especially when they're topped with spoonfuls of prepared whipped cream.

SPICY CIDER

1 quart sweet apple cider	¼ cup tiny red cinnamon candies

In saucepan, combine cider with candies. Place over campfire and heat until candies are dissolved, stirring frequently. Serve warm. Serves 4 to 5.

FIREHOUSE PUNCH

2 quarts apple juice	½ teaspoon ground cloves,
½ cup orange juice	if desired
⅓ cup cinnamon candies	

In saucepan, combine apple juice, orange juice, candies and cloves. Place over campfire and heat until candies are dissolved, stirring frequently. Serve warm. Serves 8 to 10.

Hot apple cider becomes an adult drink when it's combined with spices and applejack.

MULLED CIDER

12 cups apple cider
1½ teaspoons whole cloves
1½ teaspoons whole allspice

6 sticks cinnamon
1½ cups brown sugar
1 bottle applejack

In large saucepan, combine cider with spices tied in cheese-cloth bag. Add brown sugar. Bring to boil, stirring to dissolve sugar. Simmer for about 10 minutes; add applejack. Simmer for an additional minute; remove spices. Serve hot. Serves 18.

Most campers make hot tea the easy way, using instant tea or tea bags. If you prefer a cup of tea brewed the old-fashioned way, you'll enjoy this recipe for Mint Tea.

MINT TEA

1½ tablespoons tea leaves, black or green
½ cup boiling water

10 sprigs of mint
½ cup sugar
4 cups boiling water

Place tea leaves in pot and cover with ½ cup boiling water. Swish pot around and pour off water. Place mint sprigs in pot with tea and add sugar. Fill pot with 4 cups of boiling water and steep for 7 to 8 minutes, pushing mint down so it doesn't float above water level. Add extra sugar to taste. Serves 4.

17
Camp
Cooking Hints

. . . IF YOU CAMP where the altitude is 3,000 feet or more above sea level certain adjustments should be made in recipes and in baking temperatures. Higher altitude means lower atmospheric pressure which in turn means faster evaporation of water. Use more water in cooking and allow more time for water to boil. If you're baking with a packaged mix, follow the directions for high-altitude baking.

. . . A couple of strips of bacon in the bottom of your meat loaf pan keeps it from sticking or burning and adds flavor.

. . . For a quick and delicious cake icing, heat solid honey so it spreads easily. Spoon it over cake and sprinkle with chopped nuts.

. . . When you wrap iced cakes with waxed paper, lightly grease the paper which touches the icing and it won't stick.

. . . To make bread dough in camp, let it rise in a plastic bag, then punch down and knead dough in the bag.

. . . Lettuce won't rust if stored in a paper towel or napkin to absorb moisture and then placed in your camp cooler or refrigerator in a paper bag.

. . . To cut sticky fruits like raisins or dates, heat the knife or scissors first.

. . . If you're using instant minced onion, and you want to add it uncooked to a salad or a sandwich filling, rehydrate it before using. Add an equal amount of water to the required minced onion and let the mixture stand for about 10 minutes. The water will be absorbed, plumping up the onion bits.

. . . To whip evaporated milk, freeze the milk to form ice crystals, then whip.

. . . To measure shredded cheese, pack the cheese into the measuring cup. Four ounces of shredded cheese will fill a 1-cup measure.

. . . Before grilling, brush meat with light coating of cooking oil to prevent sticking; then grill.

. . . To make packaged puddings creamier, place waxed paper on top of hot pudding before cooling. Remove paper before serving.

. . . Cinnamon mixed with sugar is good on toast, pancakes or quick breads.

. . . Colored sugar, tinted with food coloring, is fun to use decorating camp-baked cakes or cookies.

. . . Cook meat, eggs and cheese at a moderately low heat to keep them from becoming tough.

. . . Wash fresh vegetables thoroughly, but do not soak, and cook them whole with the skins on whenever possible. Cook them quickly, covered, in a small amount of water.

. . . Heat canned vegetables in their own liquid from the can. Save leftover liquid for sauces, gravies, soups or canned soups.

. . . Wrap and store food properly: cover cut surfaces with plastic film or waxed paper and foil; close cereal packages and bread wrappings completely. This prevents spoilage and keeps insects and animals out.

. . . To clean a Teflon-lined utensil that has a film of food residue on it, use 2 tablespoons of baking soda and ½-cup liquid household bleach in 1 cup of water. Heat ingredients in utensil to boiling and simmer five minutes. Wash thoroughly, rinse and rub with oil before reusing.

. . . To remove burned food from casserole dishes, fill with warm water, add a spoonful of baking soda, soak, then wash as usual.

. . . A few pieces of chalk in trailer drawers or storage cabinets will absorb moisture and help prevent mildew. This isn't a camp-cooking hint, but it's a handy piece of advice anyway.

. . . To put out a grease fire, use baking soda or salt to suffocate the flames.

. . . Although canned foods may not spoil for years, their flavor and nutritive qualities grow less the longer they are kept. For long-term storage, consider these guidelines:

6 MONTHS:	evaporated milk, condensed meat and beef soups, dried fruit in metal containers, canned citrus fruit and juices, canned berries.
12 MONTHS:	canned fish, hydrogenated fats and oils, flour, ready-to-eat dry cereals stored in metal containers, uncooked cereal in original container, canned nuts, instant puddings, instant dry cream and bouillon products, soda and baking powder.
18 MONTHS:	canned meat, poultry and vegetables except tomatoes and sauerkraut, canned fruit except citrus fruit and juices, and berries.
24 MONTHS:	salt, whole pepper, granulated sugar.

. . . Refrigerated fresh meat should be used within two or three days, ground meat within 24 hours. In a refrigerator of 38° to 40° F., store:

Beef, veal, pork, lamb: *2 to 4 days*

Ground beef, veal, lamb, pork and variety meats: *1 to 2 days*

Luncheon meats, fresh pork sausage: *1 week*

Smoked sausage: *3 to 7 days*

Sausage, dry and unsliced: *2 to 3 weeks*

Frankfurters: *4 to 5 days*

Bacon: *5 to 7 days*

Smoked ham, whole: *1 week*

Ham slices: *3 to 4 days*

Corned beef: *7 days*

Leftover cooked meat: *4 to 5 days*

. . . To sauté fish, dip the fish in milk, coat lightly with flour, cook in hot cooking oil in large skillet. Don't place too many fish in one pan or they won't cook correctly.

. . . If you've frozen your catch, cook it frozen, don't thaw. Fish is juicier when you bake, broil, boil or steam it in the frozen state. Remember, however, to double the cooking time for frozen fish.

. . . About 3 ounces of cooked, boneless fish makes an average serving. The following table can help you decide how much fish to buy per serving.

whole fish: ¾ pound   portions: ⅓ pound
pan-dressed: ½ pound sticks: ¼ pound
fillets: ⅓ pound   canned: ⅛ pound
steaks: ⅓ pound

SUBSTITUTIONS

. . . If a recipe calls for cake flour and all you have is all-purpose flour, sift the flour and measure ½ cup. Remove one level tablespoon from the measured amount and you'll have the equivalent of ½ cup cake flour.

. . . When the recipe calls for the juice of 1 medium-size lemon, use three tablespoons of bottled lemon juice.

. . . If you need the juice of one orange, measure ½ cup of bottled orange juice.

. . . One package of active dry yeast is interchangeable with one cake of compressed yeast.

. . . To substitute for sugar, use the following measurements: For 1 cup of sugar, use: 1 cup firmly packed brown sugar; or 1 cup molasses, syrup or honey plus ½ teaspoon baking soda— then reduce the liquid in the recipe by ¼ cup; or 1½ cups maple syrup and reduce the liquid in the recipe by ¼ cup.

. . . Substitute powdered milk for fresh, following the directions on the package.

. . . When using dry herbs, 1 teaspoon of dried equals 3 tablespoons of fresh herbs.

. . . Substitute bacon-flavored vegetable protein bits in place of fresh bacon—especially good in casseroles and egg dishes.

. . . The best substitute of all—instead of doing the cooking yourself, let your husband or children substitute for you!

COOKING TERMS

Baking and Roasting means to cook with dry heat. In camp, this can be done with a reflector oven, a Dutch oven, a portable camp oven or a galley oven.

Boiling means to cook in water with the water temperature at 212° F. This is easily done in camp by using heat from a campfire, a portable camp stove or a galley range.

Braising is to brown food in a small amount of fat over a flame, then to add a small amount of water. Cooking may be continued on top of the range or in an oven in a covered utensil. Dutch ovens are especially handy for braising food.

Broiling or Grilling means to cook over direct heat—use your campfire or charcoal grill.

Deep-Fat Frying is to cook in deep fat at a high heat. Use your Dutch oven or a deep kettle placed on your camp stove or galley range.

Pan Frying is to cook in a small amount of fat on top of your range—either on your portable camp stove or your galley range.

Pressure Cooking is a method using a special utensil in which food is subjected to higher pressures than ordinary atmosphere. The advantages of cooking vegetables in a pressure cooker are that the length of cooking time is reduced, and the nutrients and flavor are conserved. For a similar effect, cook foods in tightly sealed packages of alumnium foil.

Here's a handy reference to frequently used measuring terms:

3 teaspoons	=	1 tablespoon
2 tablespoons	=	1 fluid ounce
4 tablespoons	=	¼ cup
8 tablespoons	=	½ cup
16 tablespoons	=	1 cup or 8 fluid ounces
2 cups	=	1 pint or 16 fluid ounces
4 cups	=	1 quart or 32 fluid ounces
4 quarts	=	1 gallon
4 ounces	=	¼ pound
16 ounces	=	1 pound
1 pound butter	=	2 cups
1 stick butter	=	½ cup

Common Can Sizes

INDUSTRY TERM	APPROXIMATE NET WEIGHT	APPROXI- MATE CUPS	PRODUCTS USED FOR:
8 ounce	8 ounce	1 cup	fruits and vegetables
picnic	10½ to 12 ounce	1¼ cups	condensed soups, fruits, vegetables, meat and fish
12 ounce vacuum	12 ounce	1½ cups	vacuum-packed corn
No. 300	12 to 16 ounce	1¾ cups	pork and beans, baked beans, meat products, cranberry sauce, blueberries, macaroni, spaghetti

No. 303	16 to 17 ounce	2 cups	fruits, vegetables, meat products, ready-to-serve soup
No. 2	1 pound, 4 ounce or 1 pint, 2 fluid ounce	2½ cups	juices, ready-to-serve soup, fruits and vegetables, specialties*
No. 2½	1 pound, 13 ounce	3½ cups	fruits, some vegetables
No. 3 Cylinder	3 pound, 3 ounce or 1 quart, 14 fluid ounce	5¾ cups	fruits and vegetable juices, pork and beans, institutional vegetables
No. 10	6½ pound to 7 pound, 5 ounce	12 to13 cups	fruits and vegetables for restaurants and institutional use

* Canned specialties including macaroni, spaghetti, Spanish rice, Chinese foods, etc.

INDEX

All shook up, 232
Aloha ribs, 80
Aluminum foil, 27-29
  bread recipes, 46
  chestnuts in, 49
  fish recipes, 45
  fruit recipes, 47-48
  meat recipes, 39-41
  poultry recipes, 42-45
  vegetable recipes, 29-38
Appetizers, *see* Snacks
Apple cake, quick, 200
Apple crisp, 65
Apple juice 'n tea, 240
Apples:
  campfire, 219
  caramel, 220
  cheese, 64, 219
  chilled apple dessert, 213
  cinnamon, 213
  foil-roasted, 49
  fried, 214
  Johnny Appleseed's beans, 37
  sugar, 219
Applesauce, elegant, 214
Applesauce spice cake, 198
Apricot sauce, 114

Avocado-crab treat, 223

Baby turkey in foil, 44
Bacon and bean stew, 71
Bacon rolls, 221
Bacon snack variations, 222
Bacon and tomato sandwiches, 167
Baked beans, Canadian, 157
Baked fish, 63
Baked potatoes in foil, 31
Baked sweet potatoes, 32
Banana delight, 67
Banana salad, 131
Banana salad dressing, 131
Banana shortcake, 210
Bananas, roast, 47
Barbecued chicken, 187
Barbecued chicken in foil, 42
Barbecued flank steak, 176
Barbecued pot roast, 75
Barbecued ribs, 81, 184
Barbecue rice, 37
Barbecue sauces, 174-76; *see also under* Sauces

Basic barbecue sauce, 174
Basic pot roast, 75
BBQ bread, 46
Bean and bacon stew, 71
Beans:
    campfire, 36
    Canadian baked, 157
    chuck wagon salad, 121
    Dutch oven, 87
    and franks, 61
    Johnny Appleseed's, 37
    kidney bean salad, 122
    limas and bacon, 137
    pioneer baked, 87
    three-bean salad, 121
    see also Green beans
Beef:
    barbecue, 76
    barbecued pot roast, 75
    basic pot roast, 75
    camper's chop suey, 161
    camper's treasure, 157
    Cherokee casserole, 79
    chuck wagon steak, 40
    corned, with cabbage, 149
    Dutch oven short ribs, 77
    easy beef pie, 148
    flank steak, 77
    foil surprise, 42
    grilled short ribs, 179
    grilling time, 171-72
    instant casserole, 149
    marinated beef kabobs, 191
    Mulligan stew, 74
    onion roast, 40
    pot roast, 39
    settler's stew, 73
    skillet meat pie, 158
    skillet steak supper, 160
    speedy chuck barbecue, 179

Stroganoff, 160
    two-pound hot pot, 73
    see also Ground beef; Frank-
        furters; Hamburgers; Steak;
        Stews and Casseroles
Beef liver, skillet, 161
Beef-mac casserole, 150
Beef and noodle casserole, 152
Beefed-up juice, 240
Beverages, cold:
    all shook up, 232
    apple juice 'n tea, 240
    beefed-up juice, 240
    camp lemonade, 239
    camp milk shake, 233
    Carol's punch, 238
    cherry-ale, 238
    choco-cherry milk, 233
    choco-mint milk, 232
    energy cocktail, 240
    frothy milk delight, 234
    fruit sparkler, 237
    grape fizz, 236
    groovy milk, 233
    Hawaiian lime cooler, 237
    Kate's milk cooler, 234
    lemonade-tea, 239
    orange nip, 235
    orange nog, 235
    orange pick-me-up, 239
    peanut butter delight, 232
    peppermint milk, 234
    purple potion, 236
    quick lemon-mint tea, 237
    quick orange cooler, 237
    raspberry cooler, 238
    raspberry royal, 236
    slow sipper, 238
Beverages, hot:
    campfire cocoa, 243

campfire coffee, 241
co-coffee, 242
coffee cocoa, 242
firehouse punch, 244
mint tea, 245
mulled cider, 245
spicy cider, 244
Biscuits, *see* Breads, Biscuits, Muffins
Blackberry jam cake, 196
Blackberry pie, 205
Blueberry muffins, 56
Blueberry skillet dessert, 209
Blueberry slump, 92
Bologna roll-ups, 221
Breads, Biscuits, Muffins:
  BBQ bread, 46
  butterscotch buns, 99
  cheese rolls, 101
  cream of tartar biscuits, 57
  dessert tidbits, 67
  foil-baked breads, 46
  herb dinner bread, 46
  nutty bread, 56
  onion biscuits, 90
  quick date bread, 55
  quick raisin treats, 99
  raisin wreath, 101
  reflector muffins, 56
  reflector oven corn bread, 58
  scout biscuits, 89
  scratch biscuits, 89
  sourdough bread, 103, 104
  see also Breakfast cakes; Cobblers; Corn bread
Breakfast cakes:
  breakfast cake, 54
  cinnamon cake, 55
  peanut coffee cake, 102
  pear cake, 100

quick coffee cake, 99
  raisin wreath, 101
  speedy coffee cake, 54
Bubbly noodles, 155
Bucking broncos, 63
Buttermilk dressing, 128
Butterscotch buns, 99
Butterscotch munchers, 218

Cabbage:
  corned beef casserole, 149
  crispy kraut, 123
  how to buy, 119
  see also Cole slaw
Cake icing, quick, 246
Cake mixes, recipes using, 197-201
Cakes:
  applesauce spice, 198
  blackberry jam, 196
  chocolate cream, 199
  crunch, 200
  double lemon, 199
  dressed-up Hawaiian, 199
  gingerbread-pudding, 201
  lemon surprise, 198
  orange nut, 195
  quick apple, 200
  strawberry crumble, 196
  taste of honey, 197
  walnut gingerbread, 201
  see also Breakfast cakes; Cobblers; Desserts; Pies; Snacks
Camp cooking, general hints, 246-50; *see also* Cooking techniques; Fire, building
Camper's casserole Italiano, 35
Camper's chop suey, 161

Camper's pizza, 168
Camper's rice special, 163
Camper's treasure, 157
Campfire apples, 219
Campfire beans, 36
Campfire cocoa, 243
Campfire coffee, 241
Campfire party mix, 217
Campfire potatoes and tomatoes, 142
Campfire salad, 122
Camp lemonade, 239
Camp milk shake, 233
Camp party dip, 222
Camp stove, outdoor, 14; see also Oven
Canadian baked beans, 157
Candies:
  fudge variations, 227
  marshmallow cream fudge, 227
  peanut butter fudge, 227
  quickie sweet, 228
  raisin-nut treat, 228
  shortcut fudge, 226
Cans, storage, 248
Can sizes, 251-52
Caramel apples, 220
Caramel peach crunch, 90
Carol's punch, 238
Carrot broomsticks, 118
Carrot and raisin salad, 118
Carrots:
  in foil, 29
  glazed, 138
  orange, 139
Casseroles, see Stews and Casseroles
Cereal snacks, 216
Charcoal grilling, 170-74

Cheese:
  chili cottage cheese salad, 119
  pie iron grilled, 230
  rabbit on toast, 166
  split franks and variations, 183
Cheese apples, 64, 219
Cheese-mushroom soufflé, 95
Cheese rolls, 101
Cheese soup, 106
Cheese toppers, 182
Cheesie burgers, 182
Cheesie potatoes, 33
Cheesie sauce, 113
Cheesie tomatoes, 35
Cherokee casserole, 79
Cherry-ale, 238
Cherry cobbler, 65
Cherry gems, 211
Cherry-melon salad, 131
Cherry pie, 205
Cherry shortcake doughboys, 224
  variations, 225
Chestnuts, foil-roasted, 49
Chicken:
  barbecued, 187
  Cornish hens in foil, 44
  Dutch roast, 83
  foil barbecued, 42
  grilling time for, 173
  skillet chicken delight, 162
Chicken a'roma, 187
Chicken bake, 43, 153
Chicken burgers, 166
Chicken chowder, 110
Chicken hash, 162
Chicken pie, easy, 153
Chicken salad, tangy, 127
Chicken soup, double, 105
Chicken stew, 83

Children's delight, 107
Chili beef casserole, 149
Chili beef franks, 166
Chili cottage cheese salad, 119
Chili steak, 178
Chilled apple dessert, 213
Chipper franks, 62
Choco-cherry milk, 233
Chocolate cream cake, 199
Chocolate graham pie, 204
Chocolate munchers, 218
Chocolate pecan pie, 203
Choco-mint milk, 232
Chopped meat, see Ground beef
Chop suey, camper's, 161
Chowders, see Soups; Soups, main dish
Chuck wagon salad, 121
Chuck wagon steak, 40
    marinade for, 40
Cider, mulled, 245
Cider, spicy, 244
Cinnamon apples, 213
Cinnamon cake, 55
Cobbler pie, 66
Cobblers:
    cherry, 65
    Ozark, 66
    peach, 91
    rhubarb, 91
Cocoa, campfire, 243
Co-coffee, 242
Coffee, campfire, 241
Coffee cakes:
    peanut, 102
    quick, 54, 99
    see also Breakfast cakes
Coffee cocoa, 242
"Coffee flag," 241
Cole slaw, old-fashioned, 120

Cole slaw supreme, 120
Cooking, camp, general hints, 246-50
Cooking techniques:
    aluminum foil, 27-29
    charcoal grilling, 170-74
    Dutch oven, 68-70
    fire building, 21-22
    pie iron, 229
    reflector oven 51-53
    timing of meats, 171-72
Cooking terms, definitions, 250
Corn:
    by cracky, 140
    chowder, 141
    creamed, with beans, 141
    eggs Indian style, 94
    in foil, 29, 30
    grilled, 189
    Indian, 30
    kettle, 139
    popcorn, 228, 229
    seasoned butter for, 140
    relish, 134
    tomato, 140
Corn bread:
    bucking broncos, 63
    reflector oven, 58
    sausage corn bread supper, 58
Corned beef spread, 220
Corned beef-cabbage casserole, 149
Cornflake piecrust, 204
Cornish game hens in foil, 44
Corn relish, quick, 134
Corny chowder, 141
Cottage cheese, in potato salad, 125
Country potatoes, 124
Country ribs de luxe, 81

Crabby casserole, 154
Crabmeat soup, 109
Creamed corn and beans, 141
Cream of tartar biscuits, 57
Creamy sauce, 114
Crunch cake, 200
Crunchy tuna casserole, 154
Custard, skillet, 208
Crusty crust, 204

Date bread, quick, 55
Date-nut dessert, 212
Dessert dumplings, 207
Desserts:
  apple crisp, 65
  banana delight, 67
  banana shortcake, 210
  blueberry skillet dessert, 209
  blueberry slump, 92
  campfire apples, 219
  caramel apples, 220
  caramel peach crunch, 90
  cheese apples, 64, 219
  cherry gems, 211
  cherry shortcake doughboys, 224
  chilled apple dessert, 213
  cinnamon apples, 213
  custard, 208
  date-nut dessert, 212
  dessert dumplings, 207
  dessert tidbit, 67
  Dutch rice pudding, 210
  elegant applesauce, 214
  foiled strawberries, 48
  foil peaches, 47
  foil-roasted apples, 49
  fried apples, 214
  fruit cup, 212

  fruit supreme, 212
  general discussion, 194
  kicky kabobs, 193
  lemon surprise, 198
  lemon whip, 210
  luscious pears, 192
  mincemeat oranges, 48
  open fire dessert, 208
  peach Melba shortcake, 215
  pineapple-pecan treats, 211
  poached pears, 213
  raisin-nut pears, 48
  roast bananas, 47
  s'mores, 223, 224
  snappy pudding, 211
  strawberry crumble, 196
  sugar apples, 219
  upside-down shortcake, 214
  walnut gingerbread, 201
  see also Cakes; Candies; Cobblers; Fruits; Pies; Snacks
Dessert sauces, *see* Sauces, dessert
Deviled green beans, 137
Deviled potatoes, 34
Dips:
  avocado-crab treat, 223
  camp party dip, 222
Dishwashing, outdoor, 15
Do-it-yourself salad, 126
Double chicken soup, 105
Double lemon cake, 199
Dressed-up Hawaiian cake, 199
Drinks, *see* Beverages
Dumplings, dessert, 207
Dumplings, stew, 72
Dutch Irish stew, 72
Dutch oven, 68-70
  bread and dessert recipes, 88-92

chicken recipes, 83
fish recipes, 84-85
meat recipes, 71-82
for stew-making, 70-71
vegetable recipes, 86-88
Dutch oven beans, 87
Dutch oven fish stew, 84
Dutch oven potatoes, 88
Dutch oven short ribs, 77
Dutch oven spaghetti, 79
Dutch rice pudding, 211
Dutch roast chicken, 83

Easy-does it ribs, 185
Easy Stroganoff, 160
Egg and frank salad, 127
Egg-pickle salad, 119
Egg-potato salad, hot, 124
Eggs:
    cheese-mushroom soufflé, 95
    Indian style, 94
    ranchero, 94
    three-step soufflé, 95
    Western omelet, 94
Elegant applesauce, 214
Energy cocktail, 240

Fastest sauce in the West, 113
Fire, building, 21-22
    for Dutch oven, 69-70
    for reflector oven, 52
    safety precautions, 25-26
    wood for, 22-25
    see also Charcoal grilling
Fire, grease, putting out, 248
Firehouse punch, 244

Fish and seafood:
    avocado-crab treat, 223
    baked fish, 63
    crabby casserole, 154
    crunchy tuna casserole, 154
    Dutch oven fish stew, 84
    fishermen's stew, 45
    fish Hawaiian, 189
    grilled fish, 190
    grilled trout, 188
    grilling time for, 173
    halibut pot roast, 85
    Prince Rupert halibut, 188
    seafood skillet, 163
    skillet-fried perch, 164
    tuna salad, quick, 127
    tuna surprise, 126
Fish soups:
    crabmeat, 109
    quick Pacific chowder, 109
    Sarasota chowder, 108
Flank steak, 77
Flank steak olé, 177
Foil, see Aluminum foil
Foil-barbecued chicken, 42
Foil burgers, 41
Foiled Cornish hens, 44
Foiled strawberries, 48
Foil peaches, 47
Foil pot roast, 39
Foil-roasted apples, 49
Foil-roasted chestnuts, 49
Foil surprise, 42
Food supplies, 19-20
Frankfurters:
    and beans, 61
    bucking broncos, 63
    chili beef franks, 166
    chipper franks, 62
    egg and frank salad, 127

Frankfurters, *continued*
  frank-burgers, 181
  "frankly, it's soup," 110
  frankwiches, 62
  kabob franks, 192
  and scalloped potatoes, 62
  split franks, 183
French loaf, 41
French toast, oven, 97
French toast, skillet, 96
Fried apples, 214
Frothy milk delight, 234
Fruit cup, 212
Fruits:
  apple crisp, 65
  banana delight, 67
  cheese apples, 64, 219
  chilled apple dessert, 213
  cinnamon apples, 213
  foiled strawberries, 48
  foil peaches, 47
  foil-roasted apples, 49
  fried apples, 214
  luscious pears, 192
  marshmallow fruit sandwich,
    167
  mincemeat oranges, 48
  poached pears, 213
  raisin and nut pears, 48
  roast bananas, 47
Fruit salads:
  banana, 131
  cherry-melon, 131
  fruit salad bowl, 130
  mayonnaise dressing for, 134
  Nancy's, 132
  peach-nut, 129
  sun spots, 132
Fruit sparkler, 237
Fruit supreme, 212

Garlic tomatoes, 146
Gingerbread, walnut, 201
Gingerbreat-pudding cake, 201
Gingered ham, 186
Glazed carrots, 138
Golden beef special, 159
Golden dessert sauce, 114
Grape fizz, 236
Green bean casserole, 136
Green beans:
  campfire beans, 36
  campfire salad, 122
  creamed, with corn, 141
  deviled, 137
  in foil, 30
Grilled corn, 189
Grilled fish, 190
Grilled short ribs, 179
Grilled trout, 188
Grilling, 170-74
Ground beef:
  beef-mac casserole, 150
  beef-noodle casserole, 152
  Cherokee casserole, 79
  chili beef, 149
  Dutch oven spaghetti, 79
  family rice dinner, 78
  foil surprise, 42
  French loaf, 41
  golden beef special, 159
  Kentucky burgoo, 158
  meat loaf Italiano, 60
  mushroom meat loaf, 60
  peanut sloppy Joes, 165
  quick skillet dish, 159
  Rocky Mountain burgoo, 159
  skillet steak supper, 160
  spaghetti and bones, 80
  see also Hamburgers

Hairy (coconut) squares, 226
Halibut pot roast, 85
Halibut, Prince Rupert, 188
Ham:
  gingered, 186
  ham-what-am casserole, 151
  pineapple, 59
  see also Pork and ham
Ham-apple salad, 127
  buttermilk dressing for, 128
Hamburgers:
  cheese spread for, 182
  cheesie burgers, 182
  in foil, 41
  frank-burgers, 181
  old-fashioned burgers, 180
  onion burgers, 180
  pork and beef burgers, 181
  see also Ground beef
Hardwood, see Trees
Hash, chicken, 162
Hawaiian lime cooler, 237
Herb dinner bread, 46
High-altitude timing, 246
Hollandaise, quick, 113
Honey cake, 197

Indian corn, 30
Instant casserole, 149
Instant potato casserole, 144
Italian rice loaf, 38

Jiffy pizza, 168
Johnny Appleseed's beans, 37

Kabobs:
  kabob franks, 192

kicky (dessert) kabobs, 193
  marinated beef, 191
  quick, 192
  skewered lamb, 190
Kate's milk cooler, 234
Kentucky burgoo, 158
Kettle corn, 139
Kidney bean salad, 122
Kitchen, indoor, 12-13
Kitchen, outdoor, 14-15
Kitchen equipment, 16-18
  cleaning, 17
  cooking utensils, 17-18
  disposable, 17
  outdoor, 18
  pots and pans, 16, 17
  tablewear, 17
  see also Food supplies

Lamb:
  Dutch Irish stew, 72
  grilling time, 173
  skewered kabobs, 190
  skewered supper, 191
Lemonade, camp, 239
Lemonade-tea, 239
Lemon broth, 107
Lemon cake, double, 199
Lemon chiffon pie, 202
Lemon-mint tea, 237
Lemon pancakes, 98
Lemon surprise, 198
Lemon whip, 210
Lima beans and bacon, 137
Liver, skillet, 161
Luscious pears, 192

Macaroni, bubbly, 155

Macaroni, old-fashioned, 155
Marinade for beef, 40
Marinated beef kabobs, 191
Marshmallow cream fudge, 227
Marshmallow fruit sandwich, 167
Marshmallows:
  peanut butter s'mores, 224
  s'mores, 223
  and sweet potatoes, 144
Meat loaf Italiano, 60
Meat loaves, see Ground beef
Meats:
  bologna roll-ups, 221
  corned beef spread, 220
  grilling time, 171-72
  luncheon meat kabobs, 192
  sausage corn bread supper, 58
  storage, 248
  sweet-sour skillet, 161
  see also individual names;
    Stews and casseroles;
    Ground beef; Hamburgers
Milk, see Beverages
Mincemeat oranges, 48
Mint tea, 245
Mock angel cake, 225
Mulled cider, 245
Muffins, reflector, 56; see also
    Breads, Biscuits, Muffins
Mulligan stew, 74
Mushroom meat loaf, 60
Mushrooms in foil, 30
Mustard sauce, 111

Nancy's fruit salad, 132
Nibbler's delight, 217
Noodles, bubbly, 155
Nutritional requirements, 9-11

Nutty bread, 56
Nutty salad, 123

Old-fashioned burgers, 180
Onion biscuits, 90
Onion burgers, 180
Onioned spareribs, 184
Onion roast, 40
Onions in foil, 31
Onion spuds, 143
Open fire chili peppers, 164
Open fire dessert, 208
Orange carrots, 139
Orange cooler, 237
Orange dressing, 126
Orange mini-pies, 206
Orange nip, 235
Orange nog, 235
Orange nut cake, 195
Orange pick-me-up, 239
Oranges, mincemeat, 48
Orange syrup, 96
  Oven, Dutch, see Dutch oven
Oven, outdoor, 18
Oven, portable, 14
Oven, reflector, see Reflector oven
Oven toast, 97
Ozark cobbler, 66

Pancakes, lemon, 98
Pancakes, potato, 98
Parsleyed potatoes, 142
Pastry:
  press-in butter, 202
  see also Piecrust; Pies
Peach cobbler, 91

Peaches:
    caramel peach crunch, 90
    in foil, 47
    open fire dessert, 208
Peach Melba shortcake, 215
Peach-nut salad, 129
Peanut butter delight, 232
Peanut butter fudge, 227
Peanut butter s'mores, 224
Peanut coffee cake, 102
Pear cake, 100
Pears:
    poached, 213
    raisin and nut, 48
    skewered, 192
Peas in foil, 31
Peppermint milk, 234
Peppers, open fire chili, 164
Pickle-egg salad, 119
Picnic rice, 38
Piecrust:
    crusty, 204
    packaged mix recipes, 204-06
Pie iron, how to use, 229
Pie iron grilled cheese, 230
Pie iron pizza, 230
Pie iron stew, 230
Pies:
    blackberry, 205
    cherry, 205
    chocolate graham, 204
    chocolate pecan, 203
    easy beef, 148
    easy chicken, 153
    lemon chiffon, 202
    orange mini-pies, 206
    skillet meat, 158
    strawberry, 206
Pineapple-apple relish, 135
Pineapple ham, 59

Pineapple-pecan treats, 211
Pioneer baked beans, 87
Pizza, camper's, 168
Pizza, jiffy, 168
Pizza, pie iron, 230
Pizza tomatoes, 34
Popcorn, 228, 229
Pork and beef burgers, 181
Pork chop-potato scallop, 151
Pork and ham:
    aloha ribs, 80
    bacon and bean stew, 71
    bacon rolls, 221
    bacon snack variations, 222
    barbecued ribs, 81
    country ribs de luxe, 81
    gingered ham, 186
    grilling time, 173
    ham-apple salad, 128
    ham-what-am casserole, 151
    pineapple ham, 59
    quick camper's rice, 163
    sausage corn bread supper, 58
    spaghetti and bones, 80
    sweet and sour chops, 82
    zesty sausage casserole, 156
    see also Sausage; Frankfurters;
        Spareribs
Potato casserole, instant, 144
Potatoes:
    baked in foil, 31, 32, 41
    campfire potatoes and toma-
        toes, 142
    cheesie, 33
    country, 124
    deviled, 34
    Dutch oven scalloped, 88
    and franks, 62, 156
    hot egg-potato salad, 124
    onion spuds, 143

Potatoes, *continued*
  parsleyed, 142
  pork chop-potato scallop, 151
  quick potato salad, 125
  roadside spuds, 145
  skillet scalloped, 143
  sweet, in foil, 32
  sweet, with marshmallows, 144
Potato pancakes, 98
Potato soufflé, 144
Potpourri (soup), 106
Pot roast:
  barbecued, 75
  basic, 75
  in foil, 39
Pots and pans, 16, 17
  Dutch oven, 68-70
Poultry, grilling time, 173
  see also Chicken; Turkey
Poultry sauce, 112
Prince Rupert halibut, 188
Purple potion, 236

Quick apple cake, 200
Quick barbecue sauce, 175
Quick camper's rice, 163
Quick coffee cake, 99
Quick corn relish, 134
Quick date bread, 55
Quick Hollandaise, 113
Quickie sweet, 228
Quick kabobs, 192
Quick lemon-mint tea, 237
Quick orange cooler, 237
Quick Pacific chowder, 109
Quick parsleyed potatoes, 142
Quick potato salad, 125
Quick raisin treats, 99

Quick Russian dressing, 133
Quick skillet dish, 159
Quick tuna salad, 127

Rabbit on toast, 166
Raisin and nut pears, 48
Raisin-nut treat, 228
Raisin treats, quick, 99
Raisin wreath, 101
Raspberry cooler, 238
Raspberry royal, 236
Really good dressing, 130
Reflector muffins, 56
Reflector oven corn bread, 58
Reflector ovens, 51-53
  cake and bread recipes, 54-57
  dessert recipes, 64-67
  fish recipes, 63
  meat recipes, 58-63
Refrigerators, 13, 14
Relishes:
  corn, 134
  pineapple-apple, 135
  uncooked tomato, 134
Rhubarb cobbler, 91
Rice:
  barbecue, 37
  camper's rice special, 163
  family rice dinner, 78
  Italian rice loaf, 38
  picnic rice, 38
  quick camper's, 163
  scout, 86
Rice pudding, Dutch, 211
Roadside spuds, 145
Rocky Mountain burgoo, 159
Rosy soup, 108
Russian dressing, quick, 133

Salad dressings:
 banana, 131
 buttermilk, 128
 low-calorie orange, 126
 mayonnaise variations, 134
 really good dressing, 130
 Russian, 133
 seafood, 112
 tomato-blue cheese, 133
 see also Sauces
Salads, 116, 117-31
 banana, 131
 campfire, 122
 carrot broomsticks, 118
 carrot and raisin, 118
 cherry-melon, 131
 chuck wagon, 121
 chili cottage cheese, 119
 cole slaw supreme, 120
 crispy kraut, 123
 do-it-yourself, 126
 egg and frank, 127
 fruit salad bowl, 130
 ham-apple, 128
 kidney bean, 122
 Nancy's fruit, 132
 nutty, 123
 old-fashioned cole slaw, 120
 peach-nut, 129
 pickle-egg, 119
 potato, 124, 125
 scout, 118
 sun spots, 132
 tangy chicken, 127
 three-bean, 121
 tuna, quick, 127
 tuna surprise, 126
 Vitamin C, 117
 Western, 117

Sandwiches, hot:
 broiled bacon and tomato, 167
 camper's pizza, 168
 chicken burgers, 166
 chili beef franks, 166
 jiffy pizza, 168
 marshmallow fruit, 167
 peanut sloppy Joes, 165
 rabbit on toast, 166
Sarasota chowder, 108
Sauces:
 basic barbecue, 174
 cheese toppers, 182
 cheesie, 113
 creamy, 114
 fastest in the West, 113
 mild barbecue, 175
 mustard, 111
 poultry, 112
 quick Hollandaise, 113
 seafood, 112
 seasoned corn butter, 140
 simple barbecue, 175
 Southern barbecue, 176
 Texas barbecue, 176
 tomato, 111
 see also Sauces, dessert;
  Relishes; Salad
  dressings
Sauces, dessert:
 apricot, 114
 golden dessert, 114
 orange, 126
Sausage:
 casserole, zesty, 156
 corn bread supper, 58
 quick camper's rice, 163
 two-pound hot pot, 73
 see also Frankfurters; Pork
  and ham

Scalloped potatoes, 33
  Dutch oven, 88
  skillet, 143
Scout biscuits, 89
Scout rice, 86
Scout salad, 118
Scout soup, 106
Scratch biscuits, 89
Seafood, *see* Fish and Seafood
Seafood dressing, 112
Seafood skillet, 163
Seasoned corn butter, 140
Settler's stew, 73
Shortcake:
  banana, 210
  peach Melba, 215
  upside-down, 214
Shortcut fudge, 226
Skewered lamb kabobs, 190
Skewered lamb supper, 191
Skillet chicken delight, 162
Skillet French toast, 96
Skillet fried perch, 164
Skillet liver, 161
Skillet meat pie, 158
Skillet steak supper, 160
Skillet zucchini, 146
Slow sipper, 238
S'mores, 223
Snacks:
  bacon roll, 221
  bacon variations, 222
  butterscotch munchers, 218
  campfire apples, 219
  campfire party mix, 217
  caramel apples, 220
  cereal, 216
  cheese apples, 219
  cherry shortcake doughboys, 224

  chocolate munchers, 218
  corned beef spread, 220
  dips for, 222-23
  general suggestions, 218
  hairy squares, 226
  mock angel cake, 225
  nibbler's delight, 217
  peanut butter s'mores, 224
  popcorn, 228, 229
  s'mores, 223
  sugar apples, 219
  sugar cakes, 225
Snappy pudding, 211
Softwood, *see* Trees
Soufflés:
  cheese-mushroom, 95
  potato, 144
  three-step, 95
Soups:
  cheese, 106
  children's delight, 107
  corny chowder, 141
  double chicken, 105
  lemon broth, 107
  Oriental, 107
  potpourri, 106
  Provençal, 107
  rosy, 108
  scout, 106
  see also Soups, main dish
Soups, main dish:
  chicken chowder, 110
  crabmeat, 109
  "frankly, it's soup," 110
  quick Pacific chowder, 109
  Sarasota chowder, 108
  vegetable kettle, 109
  vegetable noodle potage, 110
Sour cream beef casserole, 152
Sourdough bread, 104

starter, 103
Southern barbecue sauce, 176
Spareribs:
  Aloha ribs, 80
  barbecue, 184
  country, 81
  easy-does-it, 185
  how to buy, 183
  onioned, 184
  spicy, 185
  sweet-sour, 185
Spaghetti, Dutch oven, 79
Spaghetti and bones, 80
Speedy chuck barbecue, 179
Speedy coffee cake, 54
Spicy cider, 244
Spicy ribs, 185
Split franks, 183
Squash:
  in foil, 32
  stuffed, 32
  zucchini, 36, 146
Steak:
  chili, 178
  chuck wagon, 40
  flank, barbecued, 176
  flank, Dutch oven, 77
  flank, olé, 177
  preparation for grilling, 174
  speedy chuck barbecue, 179
Stews and casseroles:
  bean and bacon, 71
  beef-mac casserole, 150
  bubbly noodles, 155
  camper's casserole Italiano, 35
  camper's rice special, 163
  Cherokee casserole, 79
  chicken bake, 153
  chicken stew, 83
  chili beef casserole, 149

corned beef-cabbage casserole,
    149
  crunchy tuna casserole, 154
  deviled green beans, 137
  dumplings for stew, 72
  Dutch Irish stew, 72
  Dutch oven fish stew, 84
  fishermen's stew, 45
  golden beef special, 159
  ham-what-am casserole, 151
  instant casserole, 149
  instant potato casserole, 144
  Kentucky burgoo, 158
  Mulligan stew, 74
  old-fashioned macaroni, 155
  pie iron stew, 230
  pork chop-potato scallop, 151
  potatoes and franks, 156
  quick skillet dish, 159
  Rocky Mountain burgoo, 159
  settler's stew, 73
  skillet chicken delight, 162
  sour cream beef-noodle, 152
  two-pound hot pot, 73
  zesty sausage casserole, 156
  see also Soups, main dish
Storage:
  canned foods, 248
  meats, fresh, 248
  in outdoor kitchen, 15
Strawberries, foiled, 48
Strawberry crumble, 196
Strawberry pie, 206
String beans, see Green beans
Sugar apples, 219
Sugar cakes, 225
Sun spots, 132
Sweet potatoes in foil, 32
Sweet potatoes with marshmal-
    lows, 144

Sweet and sour chops, 82
Sweet-sour skillet, 161
Sweet-sour ribs, 185

Tableware, 17
Tangy chicken salad, 127
Taste of honey cake, 197
Teflon, how to clean, 247
Texas barbecue sauce, 176
Three-bean salad, 121
Three-step soufflé, 95
Tomato-blue cheese dressing, 133
Tomato corn, 140
Tomatoes:
  cheesie, 35
  in foil, 33
  garlic, 146
  pizza, 34
Tomato relish, uncooked, 134
Tomato sauce, 111
Trees:
  coniferous, 23, 25
  deciduous, 22, 23, 24-25
Trout, barbecued, 45
Trout, grilled, 188
Tuna casserole, 154
Tuna surprise, 126
Turkey, baby, 44
Turkey, grilling time, 173

Two-pound hot pot, 73

Uncooked tomato relish, 134
Upside-down shortcake, 214

Vegetable kettle, 109
Vegetable noodle potage, 110
Vegetables:
  camper's casserole Italiano, 35
  camper's treasure, 157
  in cream sauce, 147
  in foil, 29-38
  sauces for, 113
  zucchini creole, 36
  see also under individual
    names; Salads
Vitamin C salad, 117

Walnut gingerbread, 201
Western omelet, 94
Western salad, 117
Wiener wurstchen, 61; see also
  Frankfurters

Zucchini creole, 36
Zucchini, skillet, 146
Zesty sausage casserole, 156